BURGERS

BURGERS

60 tasty recipes for perfect patties, from beef to bean

RYLAND PETERS & SMALL
LONDON • NEW YORK

Senior Designer Toni Kay
Senior Editor Abi Waters
Head of Production Patricia Harrington
Art Director Leslie Harrington
Editorial Director Julia Charles

Indexer Vanessa Bird

First published in 2024
by Ryland Peters & Small
20–21 Jockey's Fields
London WC1R 4BW
and
341 E 116th St
New York NY 10029

www.rylandpeters.com

10 9 8 7 6 5 4 3 2 1

Text copyright © Miranda Ballard, Amy Ruth Finegold, Dunja Gulin, Carol Hilker, Kathy Kordalis, Jenny Linford, Dan May, Theo A. Michaels, Louise Pickford, James Porter, Shelagh Ryan, Leah Vanderveldt, Laura Washburn Hutton and Ryland Peters & Small 2024
Design and commissioned photography copyright © Ryland Peters & Small 2024
(See page 128 for full credits)

ISBN: 978-1-78879-600-2

Printed in China

A CIP record for this book is available from the British Library.
US Library of Congress Cataloging-in-Publication Data has been applied for.

NOTES
• Both British (Metric) and American (Imperial plus US cups) ingredients measurements are included in these recipes for your convenience, however it is important to work with one set of measurements and not alternate between the two within a recipe.
• All spoon measurements are level unless otherwise specified.
• All eggs are medium (UK) or large (US), unless specified as large, in which case US extra-large should be used. Uncooked or partially cooked eggs should not be served to the very old, frail, young children, pregnant women or those with compromised immune systems.
• Ovens should be preheated to the specified temperatures. We recommend using an oven thermometer. If using a fan-assisted oven, adjust temperatures according to the manufacturer's instructions.
• When a recipe calls for the grated zest of citrus fruit, buy unwaxed fruit and wash well before using. If you can only find treated fruit, scrub well in warm soapy water before using.

CONTENTS

INTRODUCTION

All hail the iconic symbol of fast-food culture, the frequently requested family treat, the ultimate fix for a hungry hangover or a bad day at work: the burger. Once solely a delicious yet formulaic American staple, now burgers are loved around the world in many different cultures and in many different forms. They are most often served as a large satisfying meal, but smaller mini burgers – known as sliders – are just as delicious and make great party food.

Clearly, the world has gone crazy for burgers and sliders, and you can find all manner of gourmet varieties in restaurants and food trucks. It has fast become the easy, failsafe option in terms of street food and satisfying snacks. The flavour combinations really are endless, taking inspiration from so many different cuisines and countries and exploring the huge range of ingredients easily at our fingertips now. The range of veggie and vegan options has also reached new heights, making a meat-free burger very easy to achieve.

Armed with this book, you don't need to trek out to an overpriced burger joint when you can quickly and easily whip up something just as good at home. The first chapter introduces some Classic, easy-to-make recipes for all-time favourite treats: don't miss the Ultimate Burger with Bacon, Cheese and Tomato Relish (see page 13) or the Deep-fried Buttermilk Chicken Burger (see page 18). Discover some new flavour sensations in the second chapter, Around the World, with tasty inventions such as the Thai Chicken Burger with Sweet Chilli Dressing (see page 49) or the Jamaican Jerk Tuna Burger with Tabasco Mayo (see page 62). Next up, try these unmissable smaller bites in the Sliders chapter, such as Malaysian Prawn Sambal Sliders (see page 70) or the Indian-style Lamb Sliders (see page 81). The Veggie and Vegan chapter provides a glorious selection of meat-free burgers – sample the Chunky Hummus Burgers (see page 89) or the Spicy Vegan Rice and Veggie Burgers (see page 93). Finally, take a peek at the Sauces and Sides chapter and choose the perfect accompaniment, from Fennel and Mint Slaw (see page 115) or Classic Hand-cut Fries (see page 119) to all manner of sauces to serve alongside your burgers, from Chilli Ketchup (see page 111) and Hot and Smoky Barbecue Sauce (see page 114) to creamy Pesto Mayo (see page 113).

Whether you are after a mean meaty tower or a light and delicious vegan number, you can find your perfect patty right here in these pages. Serve the simple recipes as weeknight dinners, slinky sliders are perfect for entertaining friends, and you could even use a gourmet recipe to woo someone special... after all, the ability to make a great burger says a lot about a person!

MAKING, SHAPING & COOKING

There's a reason that burgers have become associated with fast food, and that is because they are so easy to make and simple to cook. This has never meant that the ingredients need to be poor quality, but the time it takes to make burgers – even from scratch – is very quick. After selecting good-quality meat and other ingredients, the rest is very simple.

1. Get stuck in. Put the ingredients in a bowl and work them together with your hands. This will ensure that the ingredients are mixed together properly, as well as binding the mixture together much better than you would be able to using a food processor.

2. Squeeze. There are ingredients such as egg and breadcrumbs in these recipes, where needed, to help bind the mixture together. However, the best binding is achieved by squeezing the burgers with your hands before cooking. Really clench the ingredients together and then flatten into a patty shape – the tighter the better. It won't make the texture of the burger less fluffy. It's only the quality of the meat that dictates that.

3. Oven, fry or grill? If there are a lot of chunky ingredients in the mixture, like there are in the Beef, Goat Cheese and Bean Burger, you're going to be safer to oven-cook the burger to make sure it keeps its form. Simpler burger mixtures that bind together more easily, such as the Classic Beef Burger, are better fried or grilled/broiled.

4. What size? The good thing about making burgers yourself is that you can make them any size you like – just remember to allow a little extra cooking time for the bigger ones.

CHAPTER 1

CLASSICS

340 g/12 oz. lean minced/
ground beef

1 tbsp olive or vegetable oil,
for frying

a large pinch of sea salt and
freshly ground black pepper

Tomato relish

1 tbsp olive oil

1 onion, sliced

1 garlic clove, crushed

1 fresh red chilli/chile, chopped

800 g/3½ cups canned chopped
tomatoes

200 ml/¾ cup red wine vinegar

200 g/1 cup sugar

30 g/3 tbsp capers, rinsed

3–4 baby gherkins, chopped

a handful of fresh coriander/
cilantro

sea salt and freshly ground
black pepper

To serve

2 slices of bacon

4 slices of Cheddar cheese

2 large burger buns

butter, for spreading

American mustard

2 pickled gherkins, thinly sliced

75 g/1 cup chopped lettuce

Classic Hand-Cut Fries
(see page 119)

MAKES 2 BURGERS

ULTIMATE BURGER
WITH BACON, CHEESE & TOMATO RELISH

*This easy recipe pairs a beef patty with all the trimmings.
Serve with fries for the ultimate burger experience.*

To make the tomato relish, heat the oil in a frying pan/skillet set
over medium heat. Add the onion, garlic and chilli and fry until
soft. Add the tomatoes and mix well. Add the vinegar and sugar
and bring to the boil. Reduce the heat and simmer for about
30 minutes. Season with salt and pepper to taste. The relish
should be the consistency of jam. Stir in the capers and gherkins
and the coriander. Taste and adjust the seasoning, if necessary.

To make the burgers, put the beef in a bowl with the salt and
pepper. Work together with your hands until evenly mixed.
Divide the beef mixture in half and shape into two burger
patties. Press each burger down to make them nice and flat.

Heat the oil in a frying pan and fry the burgers over medium-
high heat for 5 minutes on each side until cooked through.

Meanwhile, heat a separate frying pan until hot and fry the
bacon slices until crisp. Remove from the pan and set aside.

When the burgers are cooked, remove from the pan and top
each with two slices of cheese. Set aside while the cheese melts.

Slice the burger buns in half and lightly toast them. Spread
butter on the cut sides of each bun. Squeeze a little mustard
onto the base and put the cooked burgers on top. Add a
generous spoonful of tomato relish to each and top with the
bacon, gherkins and lettuce. Finish the burgers with the lids
of the buns and serve with Classic Hand-Cut Fries.

CLASSIC BEEF BURGER
WITH TOMATO KETCHUP & LETTUCE

Sometimes less is more, and a simple burger made with good-quality beef speaks for itself. It's worth making a batch of homemade Tomato Ketchup to serve with these burgers – it is so much tastier than any store-bought variety.

220 g/8 oz. lean minced/
  ground beef
2 tsp tomato purée/paste
1½ tbsp fresh breadcrumbs
1 tsp chopped fresh parsley
1 tbsp olive or vegetable oil,
  for frying
a large pinch of sea salt and freshly
  ground black pepper

To serve
2 sesame seeded burger buns
Tomato Ketchup (see page 110)
lettuce leaves
Classic Hand-Cut Fries
  (see page 119)

MAKES 2 BURGERS

Put the beef in a bowl with the tomato purée, breadcrumbs, parsley and salt and pepper. Work together with your hands until evenly mixed. Divide the beef mixture in half and shape into two burger patties. Press each burger down to make them nice and flat.

Heat the oil in a frying pan/skillet and fry the burgers over medium-high heat for 5 minutes on each side until cooked.

Slice the burger buns in half. Spread a spoonful of Tomato Ketchup on the base of each bun and put the cooked burgers on top. Put a few lettuce leaves on top of each burger and finish with the lids of the buns.

Serve with Classic Hand-Cut Fries.

450 g/1 lb. minced/ground beef
140 g/1 cup onion, minced
2 garlic cloves, crushed

Dijonnaise
2 large white onions
2 tbsp butter
400 ml/1¾ cups single/light cream
3 tbsp Dijon mustard
pinch of garlic powder
pinch of ground nutmeg
small handful of chopped flat-leaf
    parsley and tarragon
sea salt and freshly ground
    black pepper

To serve
8 slices of bacon
4 eggs
4 brioche buns
4 slices of American or Cheddar
    cheese
Spicy Dill Pickles, chopped
    (see page 124)
Sweet & Sour Cherry Pickles
    (see page 124)
Classic Hand Cut Fries
    (see page 119)
Ranch Dressing (see page 123)

Makes 4

DINER CHEESEBURGER

*According to food historians, the cheeseburger was
invented in 1920 in Pasadena, California, a remarkable
20 years after the hamburger first appeared. Lionel
Sternberger (no pun intended), a cook at his father's
sandwich shop, "The Rite Spot", one day decided
to place a slab of American cheese on a hamburger,
inventing one of the world's most loved sandwiches.*

First, make the Dijonnaise by finely chopping the white
onions and frying with the butter in a medium saucepan.
Add the cream and mix in the mustard. Season the mixture
with salt and pepper, then add the garlic powder, nutmeg
and herbs. Simmer until the sauce takes on a mustardy
colour and is relatively thick. Set aside.

Mix together the minced beef, minced onion and garlic.
Shape into patties and sprinkle with salt and pepper. Grill
to your liking.

In a medium frying pan/skillet, fry the bacon and eggs,
then set aside.

Cut a brioche bun in half and spread a layer of Dijonnaise
Place a cooked patty on top, then a slice of cheese, followed
by a fried egg, 2 slices of bacon and some chopped dill pickle.

Serve with Sweet & Sour Cherry Pickles, Classic Hand-Cut
Fries and Ranch Dressing.

DEEP-FRIED BUTTERMILK CHICKEN BURGER

'Nduja is a type of Italian salami blended with roasted red peppers into a spicy paste. If you are unable to find it, you can simply blend some chorizo sausage in a food processor until it is paste-like, which makes for a decent alternative.

8 skinless, boneless chicken thighs
250 ml/1 cup buttermilk
sunflower oil, for frying

Slaw
125 g/2 cups shredded red cabbage
100 g/³⁄₄ cup grated/shredded carrots
¹⁄₂ red onion, thinly sliced
1 tsp sea salt
1¹⁄₂ tsp caster/granulated sugar
2 tsp white wine vinegar
6 tbsp mayonnaise

Coating
100 g/³⁄₄ cup plain/all-purpose flour
1 tsp sea salt
1 tsp mustard powder
¹⁄₂ tsp smoked paprika
¹⁄₂ tsp celery salt
¹⁄₄ tsp freshly ground black pepper

To serve
4 brioche burger buns
125 g/4 oz. 'nduja sausage
a handful of lettuce leaves

SERVES 4

Cut the chicken thigh fillets in half and place in a shallow dish. Pour over the buttermilk, cover and chill overnight. This will tenderize the chicken. The next day, remove the chicken from the fridge and return to room temperature for 30 minutes.

Make the slaw. Combine the cabbage, carrots and onion with the salt, sugar and vinegar and set aside for 30 minutes. Drain the cabbage mixture and combine with the mayonnaise.

Preheat the oven to 180°C (350°F) Gas 4.

Make the coating. In a bowl, combine the flour with the salt, mustard powder, smoked paprika, celery salt and black pepper.

Carefully remove the chicken thighs from the buttermilk and immediately dip into the flour mixture, making sure they are completely coated.

Heat 5 cm/2 inches of sunflower oil in a saucepan to 190°C (375°F) or until a cube of bread browns in 30 seconds. Deep-fry the coated chicken pieces for 3–4 minutes on each side until crisp and golden. Transfer them to the oven to keep warm while cooking the rest.

To serve, cut the buns in half and lightly toast the cut sides under the grill/broiler. Fill with the chicken fritters and add some 'nduja, lettuce and slaw. Serve at once, with Sweet Potato Fries, if you like (see page 120).

ROAST GARLIC PORK BURGERS

Making your own burgers is very simple and allows you to be creative with the flavourings. Adding roast garlic, fennel seeds and lemon zest gives a great depth of flavour to these tasty burgers, perfect for summertime barbecues. Serve with fries and crunchy coleslaw.

1 head of garlic, top sliced off
to expose the cloves

½ tsp fennel seeds

400 g/14 oz. minced/ground pork

1 tbsp finely chopped fresh parsley

1 tsp grated lemon zest

sunflower or vegetable oil,
for frying

salt and freshly ground
black pepper

4 brioche rolls or hamburger buns,
halved

mayonnaise, ketchup and sliced
gherkins, as desired

SERVES 4

To roast the garlic, preheat the oven to 180°C (350°F) Gas 4. Wrap the garlic in foil and bake for 1 hour. Unwrap the foil and set aside to cool. When it is cool enough to handle, squeeze out the softened pulp from each clove and mash into a paste.

Dry-fry the fennel seeds in a frying pan/skillet until fragrant, then cool and grind.

Mix together the pork, roast garlic paste, ground fennel, parsley and lemon zest, mixing thoroughly. Season well with salt and pepper. Shape the minced pork into 4 patties.

Add a touch of oil to a large frying pan/skillet and heat through. Add the patties and fry for 15–20 minutes, or until cooked through, turning over as they cook.

Place the patties in the rolls, adding mayonnaise, ketchup and gherkins to taste and serve at once.

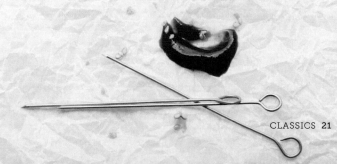

BIG BREAKFAST BURGER
WITH A PORTOBELLO MUSHROOM & A FRIED EGG

A hearty pork burger with all the traditional breakfast trimmings – for the days when cereal just won't cut it.

2 tbsp olive oil

5 mushrooms, finely chopped

200 g/7 oz. lean minced/ground pork

2 tsp Tomato Ketchup (see page 110), or store-bought ketchup

a pinch of mustard powder

3 tbsp fresh breadcrumbs

a pinch of sea salt and freshly ground black pepper

To serve

2 English muffins

Tomato Ketchup (see page 110), or store-bought ketchup

2 fried eggs

2 grilled/broiled Portobello mushrooms

MAKES 2 BURGERS

Heat 1 tablespoon of the oil in a frying pan/skillet set over medium heat. Add the chopped mushrooms and fry until soft and brown. Remove from the heat and set aside.

Put the pork in a bowl with the Tomato Ketchup, mustard powder, breadcrumbs and salt and pepper. Work together with your hands until evenly mixed. Add the cooled mushrooms and mix again. Divide the mixture in half and shape into two burger patties. Press each burger down to make them nice and flat.

Heat the remaining oil in the same frying pan and fry the burgers over medium-high heat for 5 minutes on each side until cooked through.

Slice the English muffins in half and lightly toast them under the grill/broiler or in the toaster. Spread a spoonful of Tomato Ketchup on the base of each muffin and put the cooked burgers on top. Put a fried egg and a grilled Portobello mushroom on top of each burger and finish with the lids of the English muffins. Serve with extra Tomato Ketchup on the side.

SOUTHERN CHICKEN BURGERS
WITH CABBAGE & LIME SLAW

This is a fondue version of fried chicken burgers. The chicken pieces are skewered with fondue forks and deep-fried at the table. Diners make their own little burgers with brioche rolls and the delicious fennel and lime slaw.

2 chicken breast fillets
125 ml/½ cup buttermilk
4 brioche burger rolls, halved
4 handfuls of salad leaves
sunflower oil, for deep-frying
Classic Mayo (see page 112),
  to serve

Cabbage & lime slaw
125 g/4½ oz. red cabbage,
  shredded
½ fennel, shredded
½ onion, thinly sliced
2 tsp freshly squeezed lime juice
1½ tsp caster/granulated sugar
1 tsp sea salt

Breadcrumb coating
100 g/1¼ cups dried breadcrumbs
1 tsp mustard powder
½ tsp sea salt
½ tsp smoked paprika
¼ tsp freshly ground black pepper

SERVES 4

Cut the chicken breasts into 3-cm/1¼-inch pieces and place in a dish. Pour over the buttermilk, cover and chill overnight to tenderize the chicken. The next day, remove the chicken from the fridge and return to room temperature for 30 minutes.

To make the slaw, place the cabbage, fennel and onion in a bowl. Combine the lime juice, sugar and salt in a separate small bowl and stir well, then add to the slaw, stirring to combine. Set aside until required.

Combine all the breadcrumb coating ingredients in a bowl. Remove the chicken pieces from the buttermilk and immediately dip into the crumb mixture, pressing down well and making sure they are totally coated. Cover and place on the table with the brioche rolls, bowls of the cabbage mix, salad leaves and some mayonnaise.

Heat enough oil to come a third of the way up the sides of a metal fondue pan until it reaches 180°C/350°F. As soon as the oil reaches temperature, very carefully transfer the pot to the tabletop burner. Diners can now skewer the chicken pieces and gently lower into the hot oil, letting them cook for 2–3 minutes until golden and cooked through. Allow to cool for a minute or two. Assemble the rolls with the fried chicken, slaw, salad leaves and Mayo, then top with the bun lids and eat.

PULLED PORK BURGERS

A long, slow cook is the perfect way to produce melt-in-the-mouth pulled pork. Served in a bun with luscious Hot & Smoky Barbecue Sauce, it's a winning combo.

3 kg/6½ lb. free-range, bone-in pork shoulder (rind on, if you would like to make crackling)

1 tbsp sea salt

3 tbsp olive oil

1 tsp paprika

a big pinch of cayenne pepper

To serve

warm brioche rolls

Hot & Smoky Barbecue Sauce (see page 114)

SERVES 10–12

Preheat the oven to 190°C (375°F) Gas 5.

If you want to make crackling, use a sharp knife to score diagonal lines across the rind and push the salt into the cuts. This draws the moisture out so that the surface crackles.

Fold a large piece of foil in two and place it in a roasting pan. You're going to need enough foil either side to cover and seal the pork. Place the pork on top. Drizzle the olive oil over the surface and sprinkle over the paprika and cayenne.

Keeping the foil open at this stage, place the meat in the oven and roast for 25 minutes so that the outside has a chance to brown. Then turn the temperature right down to 150°C (300°F) Gas 2, fold in the sides of the foil so that the meat is totally covered and cook for at least 3 hours, or 4 hours if you can. Every hour, open up the foil and baste the meat by spooning the juices from the bottom of the pan back over the top of the joint. After 3–4 hours, prod it with a fork and see if it is easy to 'pull' (the strips in the muscle should have 'melted' apart). Return for a little longer if it still feels tight.

Open the foil, increase the heat to 200°C (400°F) Gas 6 and continue to cook for 5 minutes to crisp up the top. Remove the crackling and set aside.

Use two forks to 'pull' the pork to shreds. Cut the crackling into thin strips. Serve the pork in warm brioche rolls with Hot & Smoky Barbecue Sauce and crackling on the side.

BURNT ENDS

Burnt ends are the pieces of meat cut from the narrower end of a brisket, and they are considered a delicacy in southern cooking. The high fat content means it takes longer to cook to tender, hence the term 'Burnt Ends'.

1.8 kg/4 lb. beef brisket, trimmed
375 ml/1½ cups beef stock
125–250 ml/½–1 cup Hot & Smoky Barbecue Sauce (see page 114)
125 ml/½ cup drippings from the brisket, reserved

Dry rub
2 tbsp chilli powder
2 tbsp sea salt
1 tbsp garlic powder
1 tbsp cayenne pepper
½ tsp dried oregano
1 tbsp onion powder
1 tbsp ground black pepper
1 tbsp brown sugar
2 tsp dry mustard
1 fresh bay leaf, crushed

To serve
4 burger buns, halved
Sweet Potato Fries (see page 120)
macaroni cheese, to serve
   (optional)

food smoker or barbecue

SERVES 4

Preheat the oven to 180°C (350°F) Gas 4. Combine all the dry rub ingredients together in a bowl. Season the brisket on both sides with the rub, place in a roasting pan and roast, uncovered, for 1 hour.

Add the stock and enough water so that there is about 1.25 cm/½ inches of liquid in the pan. Reduce the oven temperature to 150°C (300°F) Gas 2, cover the pan tightly and cook for 3 hours, or until fork-tender.

Remove the brisket from the oven. Trim any fat away from the brisket (reserving any dripping) and cut into 1.25 cm/½ inch cubes and place in a large disposable tray. Add in the BBQ sauce and brisket drippings. Toss thoroughly.

Prepare a smoker following the manufacturer's instructions. Place the tray in the smoker and smoke at 100°C (225°F) until the brisket pieces darken and become crisp around the edges, 30–45 minutes.

Remove from the smoker and set aside to cool for about 10 minutes.

Serve in burger buns with additional Barbecue Sauce, if desired, alongside sweet potato fries and macaroni cheese, if liked.

TURKEY BURGER
WITH ONION & CRANBERRY JAM

*Here turkey mince is flavoured with wholegrain mustard and the
cooked burger is served with delicious onion and cranberry jam/relish.*

625 g/1⅓ lb. skinless turkey breast
　fillet, coarsely chopped
125 g/4 slices of smoked streaky/
　fatty bacon, coarsely chopped
2 tbsp wholegrain mustard
2 tbsp chopped fresh flat-leaf parsley
½ tsp smoked paprika
sea salt and freshly ground
　black pepper
sunflower oil, for shallow frying

Onion & cranberry jam/relish
2 tbsp olive oil
2 red onions, thinly sliced
50 g/⅓ cup dried cranberries
1 tbsp balsamic vinegar
100 g/½ cup cranberry sauce

To serve
4 burger buns, halved
a handful of watercress

SERVES 4

To make the onion and cranberry jam, heat the oil in a
saucepan, add the onions and fry over medium heat for
20–25 minutes until caramelized, stirring occasionally.

Meanwhile, soak the cranberries in the vinegar until
required. Add the cranberries to the onions along with
the cranberry sauce and 2 tablespoons water and cook for
10 minutes until thickened and jam-like. Season to taste
with salt and pepper and set aside to cool.

Put the turkey and bacon in a food processor and blend
until coarsely minced. Transfer to a bowl, add the mustard,
parsley, paprika and some salt and pepper and work
together with your hands until evenly mixed. Cover and
chill for 30 minutes. Divide into four portions and shape
into burger patties. Press each burger down to make them
nice and flat.

Heat a shallow layer of sunflower oil in a frying pan/skillet,
add the turkey patties and fry for 4–5 minutes on each side
until cooked through. Keep them warm.

Lightly toast the buns under the grill/broiler and then fill
with watercress, patties and the onion and cranberry jam.
Serve at once.

HEALTHY COD BURGER
WITH WATERCRESS & ALMOND PESTO

Lightly salting the cod before cooking firms up the flesh, making it easier to fry and hold together, and thus more suitable for a burger. Paired with a simple watercress pesto, it's hard to believe this is a healthy dish!

4 x 150 g/6 oz. skinless boneless cod fillets

2 tsp sea salt

1 tbsp olive oil, plus extra for frying

grated zest of 1 lemon

4 sprigs thyme, leaves picked

salt and freshly ground black pepper

Watercress & almond pesto

25 g/1 oz. blanched almonds

100 g/2 cups watercress leaves

juice of 1 lemon

1 garlic clove, crushed

2 tbsp basil leaves

2 tbsp natural yogurt

1 tbsp extra virgin olive oil

To serve

4 seeded rolls

125 g/4 oz. baby plum tomatoes, halved

SERVES 4

Trim the cod fillets and remove any remaining bones. Place in a shallow bowl and add the salt, rubbing it lightly into the fish, then set aside for 2 hours in the fridge. Rinse the fish under cold water and pat dry using paper towels.

Combine the oil in a bowl with the lemon zest, thyme leaves and some salt and pepper. Rub into the fish and set aside until required.

Make the pesto. Dry fry the almonds in a small frying pan/skillet until lightly browned. Roughly chop half the watercress and place in a food processor with the almonds, lemon juice, garlic, basil, yogurt, oil and a little salt and pepper. Blend until fairly smooth.

Heat a frying pan/skillet over medium heat and fry the cod fillets for 2–3 minutes on each side until golden. Rest for 3 minutes.

Cut the rolls in half and lightly toast the cut sides under the grill/broiler. Place a fish fillet onto each base and spoon over the pesto, then add the remaining watercress leaves and the halved tomatoes. Serve at once.

BACON BURGER WITH CREAMY SLAW

Smoked bacon adds great flavour to these patties, which are equally good made with minced/ground chicken instead of beef. A creamy rosemary coleslaw is pleasantly tangy and makes a change from regular classic coleslaw.

625 g/1⅓ lb. minced/ground beef
125 g/4 oz. smoked back bacon,
    minced/ground
1 onion, finely chopped
1 garlic clove, crushed
1 tbsp freshly chopped sage leaves
1 egg yolk
1 tbsp wholegrain mustard
sea salt and freshly ground
    black pepper
olive oil, for brushing

To serve
4 poppy seed rolls, halved
4 iceberg lettuce leaves
2 tomatoes, sliced
½ recipe Rosemary Coleslaw
    (see page 116)

SERVES 4

Put the beef, bacon, onion, garlic, sage, egg yolk, mustard and some salt and pepper in a bowl and work together with your hands to form a slightly sticky mixture. Divide into four portions and shape into burger patties. Press each burger down to make them nice and flat. Cover and chill for 30 minutes.

Brush the patties lightly with olive oil and barbecue or grill/broil for 5 minutes on each side until cooked through. Keep them warm.

Lightly toast the poppy seed rolls under the grill/broiler or in the toaster and fill them with lettuce leaves, tomato slices, the patties and the Rosemary Coleslaw. Serve at once.

SUPERFOOD BURGERS

These are the ultimate superfood beef burgers, with a tasty hit of protein, iron and antioxidants, as well as vitamins A, B6 and C.

300 g/10½ oz. minced/ground beef

1 cooked beetroot/beet, grated

½ cooking apple, peeled and diced

20 g/4 tsp tomato purée/paste

1 tsp powdered spirulina (optional)

20 g/4 tsp dried breadcrumbs (optional)

1 garlic clove, finely chopped

a pinch each of salt and freshly ground black pepper

oil, for frying

To serve

wholemeal/wholewheat rolls

spinach leaves

hummus, to serve

MAKES 2

Mix the beef, grated beetroot, diced cooking apple, tomato purée, spirulina, if using, and breadcrumbs (if using), garlic, salt and pepper together with your hands until well mixed.

Divide the mixture in half and shape into two burgers, making sure they're not too fat, so that it's easier to cook them through.

Heat a little oil in a frying pan/skillet over high heat and put the burgers in. Don't turn them too quickly; let them sear fully on the first side for 4–5 minutes before you move them. Turn and cook on the other side for 5–6 minutes, until they're cooked thoroughly in the middle.

For extra goodness, serve in a lightly toasted wholemeal roll with a few spinach leaves and a dollop of hummus on the top.

BEEF, GOAT CHEESE & BEAN BURGER WITH PESTO MAYO

These classic beef burgers are given a summery twist with the addition of fresh broad beans, creamy goat cheese and a delicious pesto mayo.

15 g/1 tbsp butter

1 garlic clove, finely chopped

30 g/¼ cup shelled fresh broad/ fava beans

160 g/6 oz. lean minced/ ground beef

15 g/½ oz. goat cheese, crumbled

4 tsp tomato purée/paste

1 tbsp beaten egg

3 tbsp fresh breadcrumbs

a pinch of sea salt and freshly ground black pepper

To serve

2 wholemeal/wholewheat bread rolls

butter, for spreading

Pesto Mayo (see page 113)

watercress and radish salad (optional)

MAKES 2 BURGERS

Preheat the oven to 180°C (350°F) Gas 4.

Melt the butter in a frying pan/skillet set over medium heat and add the garlic. Add the broad beans and stir until browned. When cooked, remove from the pan, crush with a fork and set aside to cool.

Put the beef in a bowl with the goat cheese, tomato purée, egg, breadcrumbs and salt and pepper. Work together with your hands until evenly mixed. Add the crushed broad beans and mix again. Divide the mixture in half and shape into two burger patties. Press each burger down to make them nice and flat. Lay the burgers on a baking sheet and bake in the preheated oven for 20 minutes, turning halfway through cooking.

Slice the bread rolls in half and spread both cut sides of each roll with a little butter. Put a cooked burger on the bottom half of each bread roll and top with a spoonful of Pesto Mayo. Finish the burgers with the lids of the bread rolls and serve with a watercress and radish salad, if liked.

FISH PIE BURGER WITH CAPERS & TARTARE SAUCE

This fish pie in burger form is a real treat for anyone who enjoys a burger but doesn't want to eat meat. Serve with Classic Hand-Cut Fries for a hearty and sustaining meal.

250 g/9 oz. boneless salmon fillets

50 g/2 oz. cooked small prawns/ shrimp

30 g/¹/₃ cup fresh breadcrumbs

1 tbsp beaten egg

1 tbsp capers, chopped

1 garlic clove, finely chopped

1 tsp finely grated Parmesan cheese

a good pinch of freshly chopped chives

a good pinch of freshly chopped parsley

a pinch of sea salt and freshly ground black pepper

To serve

2 sesame or plain bagels

tartare sauce

a handful of baby spinach leaves

Classic Hand-Cut Fries (see page 119)

MAKES 2 LARGE BURGERS

Preheat the oven to 180°C (350°F) Gas 4.

Put the salmon fillets in a greased baking dish and bake in the preheated oven for 20 minutes, turning halfway through cooking. Remove from the oven and set aside until cool enough to handle. Leave the oven on.

Put the prawns in a bowl with the breadcrumbs, egg, capers, garlic, Parmesan, chives, parsley and salt and pepper. Work together with your hands until evenly mixed. Remove the skin from the salmon and break it up into flakes, add to the bowl and mix again. Divide the mixture in half and shape into two burger patties. Press each burger down to make them nice and flat.

Lay the burgers on a baking sheet and bake in the preheated oven for 15–20 minutes, turning halfway through cooking.

Slice each bagel in half and lightly toast them under the grill/ broiler or in the toaster. Spread the bottom half of each bagel with tartare sauce. Put a cooked burger on top and cover with a few baby spinach leaves. Finish the burgers with the lids of the bagels and serve with Classic Hand-Cut Fries.

CHAPTER 2

AROUND
THE WORLD

ITALIAN BURGER
WITH OLIVES, SUN-DRIED TOMATOES & PESTO

With all the flavours of Italy, this hearty and heavenly burger will transport your tastebuds to an Italian lakeside table adorned with Chianti and candlelight.

220 g/8 oz. lean minced/ground beef
4 pitted black olives, finely chopped
2 sun-dried tomatoes, finely chopped
2 tsp tomato purée/paste
2 tsp pesto
a pinch of sea salt and freshly ground black pepper

To serve
2 ciabatta rolls
Pesto Mayo (see page 113)
a bowl of black olives (optional)

MAKES 2 BURGERS

Preheat the grill/broiler to medium.

Put the beef in a bowl with the olives, sun-dried tomatoes, tomato purée, pesto and salt and pepper. Work together with your hands until evenly mixed. Divide the beef mixture in half and shape into two burger patties. Press each burger down to make them nice and flat.

Put the burgers on a baking sheet and grill/broil for 5 minutes on each side until cooked through. Remove from the grill/broiler and set aside. Leave the grill on.

Slice the ciabatta rolls in half and lightly toast them under the hot grill.

Put a cooked burger on the bottom half of each ciabatta roll and top with a large spoonful of pesto mayo. Finish the burgers with the lids of the ciabatta rolls and serve with a bowl of olives on the side, if liked.

500 g/1 lb. 2 oz. minced/ground
  lamb (lean is good but a little fat
  is better as this helps to create
  a juicy burger)
1 small onion, finely chopped
½ small eating apple, peeled,
  cored and grated
5 sun-dried apricots, finely
  chopped
1 garlic clove, crushed
1 small red chilli/chile, deseeded
  and finely chopped
1½ tsp ras el hanout
  (Moroccan spice blend)
1 tbsp chilli jam/pepper jelly
1 tbsp plain/all-purpose flour
1 tbsp sunflower oil
sea salt and freshly ground
  black pepper

Yogurt dressing
½ small red onion, thinly sliced
4 tbsp plain yogurt
small handful of fresh mint,
  finely chopped
100 g/½ cup finely chopped
  pickles
good squeeze of lemon juice

To serve
toasted pita bread
simple salad

SERVES 6

MOROCCAN-SPICED LAMB BURGERS WITH YOGURT DRESSING

*A good, spiced lamb burger can always be improved by
the addition of a fruity element; in this case grated apple
and dried apricots work so well with the other flavours.*

To make the burgers, put the lamb, onion, apple, apricots, garlic,
chilli, ras el hanout, chilli jam, 1 teaspoon salt and 1 teaspoon
pepper in a large bowl. Work together with your hands until
evenly mixed. Try to mix it evenly without overworking the
mixture. It should now just hold together. Divide the mixture
into 6 and gently press to flatten and form generous burgers.

Place the burgers on a lightly floured tray, cover with cling film/
plastic wrap and refrigerate for at least 1 hour. The flavours will
benefit from being left to meld for longer.

Meanwhile, to make the yogurt dressing, place the sliced
onion in a medium bowl, then pour over enough just-boiled
water to cover. Leave for about 30 seconds. Drain and rinse the
onion under cold water. Pat dry on kitchen paper and season
lightly with a little salt. Put the yogurt and mint in a small bowl
and mix together. Add the pickles, onions and lemon juice
and mix. Cover and chill until you are ready to serve.

Just before you are ready to cook the burgers, preheat a
barbecue/grill or grill/broiler to medium–hot. Brush the
sunflower oil over the burgers and barbecue or grill/broil for
6–8 minutes each side, or until they are cooked through.

Serve the burgers with toasted pita bread, a simple salad and
a dollop of the yogurt dressing.

1 tbsp peanut or vegetable oil, plus extra for cooking
1 shallot, thinly sliced
1 garlic clove, crushed
2.5-cm/1-inch piece of fresh ginger, grated
1 tsp shrimp paste (from Thai and Asian food stores)
1 tbsp desiccated/shredded coconut
1 tsp caster/granulated sugar
500 g/1 lb. 2 oz. skinless, boneless chicken thigh fillets, roughly chopped

Sweet chilli/chile dressing
1 chilli/chile, deseeded and sliced
juice of 2 limes, freshly squeezed
1 tbsp Thai fish sauce
2 tbsp caster/granulated sugar

To serve
4 rolls
a handful of Asian salad leaves
a handful of fresh herbs (e.g. Thai basil, coriander/cilantro, mint)
1 mango, peeled, stoned and sliced
2 tbsp crispy fried shallots

SERVES 4

THAI CHICKEN BURGER
WITH MANGO, CRISPY SHALLOTS & SWEET CHILLI DRESSING

A lovely homemade sweet chilli/chile dressing adds that classic Thai hot, sweet, salty and sour flavour we all love, and is a perfect foil to the chicken and mango.

Heat the oil in a wok and gently fry the shallot, garlic and ginger for 5 minutes until softened. Stir in the shrimp paste, coconut and sugar and stir-fry for 1 minute until fragrant, then continue to stir until you have a slightly sticky paste mix. Set aside to let cool.

Place the chicken pieces in a food processor with the cooled spice paste and blend until coarsely minced. Shape into 8 small burger patties. Press each burger down to make them nice and flat, then cover and chill for 30 minutes.

Meanwhile, make the chilli dressing. Place the ingredients in a bowl and whisk until the sugar is dissolved.

Heat a ridged stove-top grill pan over high heat. Brush the patties with a little oil and cook for 3–4 minutes on each side until charred and cooked through. Rest for 5 minutes.

To serve, cut the rolls almost in half and open out wide. Fill with salad leaves and herbs. Top each roll with 2 burgers and a few mango slices. Drizzle over the dressing and scatter over the crispy shallots. Serve at once.

CHILLI CON CARNE BURGER

This hearty recipe is the burger interpretation of a traditional chili con carne. These deliciously spicy burgers are just as good served on open bread rolls or simply as they are.

1 tbsp olive oil

1 large courgette/zucchini, sliced lengthways into thin strips

200 g/7 oz. lean minced/ground beef

2 tbsp chopped cooked kidney beans

4 tsp tomato purée/paste

½ red onion, finely chopped

3 tbsp fresh breadcrumbs

1 tbsp beaten egg

1 fresh red chilli/chile, finely chopped

a pinch of ground cumin

sea salt and freshly ground black pepper

To serve

4 slices of Cheddar cheese

2 wholemeal/wholewheat bread rolls (optional)

2 tbsp sour cream

Classic Hand-Cut Fries (see page 119)

MAKES 2 BURGERS

Preheat the grill/broiler to medium.

Heat the oil in a ridged stove-top grill pan. Add the courgette slices and cook over high heat, turning occasionally, until browned on each side. Set aside to cool.

Put the beef in a bowl with the kidney beans, tomato purée, onion, breadcrumbs, egg, chilli, cumin and salt and pepper. Work together with your hands until evenly mixed. Divide the beef mixture in half and shape into two burger patties. Squeeze them together to keep the ingredients well packed inside, then press each burger down to make them nice and flat.

Put the burgers on a baking sheet and grill/broil for 5 minutes on each side until cooked through. When the burgers are cooked, remove from the grill and top each with two cheese slices. Wrap a slice of grilled courgette around each burger and then fold the slices of courgette over the top so they meet in the middle.

Slice the bread rolls in half, if using, and put a wrapped burger on the bottom half of each bread roll. Serve with sour cream for spooning and Classic Hand-cut Fries on the side.

SPICY PORK BURGER

The spicy Asian flavours and sweet fresh mango salsa set this succulent pork burger apart from a traditional beef burger, and makes a lighter alternative too.

45 ml/3 tbsp olive oil

115 g/¾ cup (about 1 small) finely diced onion

3 garlic cloves, crushed

a 4-cm/1½-inch piece of ginger, peeled and finely grated

900 g/2 lb. minced/ground pork

2 long red chillies/chiles, deseeded and finely chopped

1 tbsp fish sauce

2 tbsp chopped coriander/cilantro

60 g/2 oz. bacon

2 eggs

sea salt and freshly ground black pepper, to season

To serve

6 burger buns, halved

mayonnaise

Mango Salsa (see page 115)

Fennel and Mint Slaw (see page 115)

SERVES 6

Heat 1 tablespoon of the oil in a frying pan/skillet and sauté the onion, garlic and ginger over gentle heat until soft. Remove from the heat and allow to cool.

Place the remaining ingredients in a large bowl, add the onion mixture and combine. Season with salt and pepper.

Form into 6 patties (about 180 g/ 6½ oz. each) pressing each burger down to make it nice and flat. Chill until ready to cook.

Preheat the oven to 170°C (325°F) Gas 3.

Heat the remaining 2 tablespoons of oil in a large frying pan and fry the burger patties for 4 minutes, turning once, until nice and brown on both sides. You may need to do this in batches, depending on the size of your pan.

Transfer the patties to a baking sheet and finish off by cooking in the preheated oven for a further 10 minutes.

While the patties are cooking, lightly toast the burger buns. Spread some mayonnaise on the bottom bun and top with the pork patty, mango salsa and the other half of the bun. Serve with the Fennel & Mint Slaw on the side.

TERIYAKI BURGER

Affectionately known as 'teri burgers', these are Hawai'i's take on this American classic. The teri sauce gives these burgers a sweet, sticky quality and helps to keep the meat moist and extra succulent. Although frying is the suggested cooking method here, they are arguably even better cooked on the barbecue or grilled/broiled.

450 g/1 lb. minced/ground steak

1 bunch spring onions/scallions, finely sliced (white and green parts)

1 tsp finely chopped fresh ginger

1 tsp finely chopped garlic

¼ tsp freshly ground black pepper

¼ tsp sea salt

2½ tbsp teriyaki sauce

10 g/¼ cup panko breadcrumbs

1 tbsp toasted sesame seeds

2 tbsp vegetable oil

To serve

4 burger buns, halved and warmed (brioche buns work well)

thinly sliced red onion, lettuce and tomato

your favourite ketchup (see pages 110–111)

your favourite pickles (see page 124)

MAKES 4

Place the steak in a large bowl with the spring onions, ginger, garlic, pepper, salt, teriyaki sauce, panko breadcrumbs and sesame seeds. Mix together well. Divide the mixture into four burgers and shape into round patties, approx. 2.5 cm/1 inch thick.

Heat the oil in a heavy-based frying pan/skillet over medium-high heat. Fry the burgers for about 4 minutes on each side, or for a little longer if you prefer your burger well-done.

Serve each burger in a warm bun with thinly sliced red onion, lettuce and tomato. Serve with ketchup on the side, along with your favourite pickles.

Tip For an extra tropical twist, try topping each of your burgers with a grilled/broiled pineapple ring.

MIDDLE EASTERN SLIDERS WITH TAHINI SAUCE

Lovely rich flavours combine in this Middle-Eastern style dish, where aubergine/eggplant is partnered with preserved lemon, pomegranate, tahini and ras el hanout – a classic North African spice mix.

100 g/3½ oz. semi-dried tomatoes, sliced

½ preserved lemon, flesh discarded and skin diced

4 tbsp pine nuts

4 tbsp pomegranate seeds

4 tbsp parsley leaves

3 tbsp extra virgin olive oil

2 tsp honey

1 large aubergine/eggplant (about 450 g/1 lb.)

1 tsp ras el hanout

salt and freshly ground black pepper

Tahini sauce

100 g/⅓ cup Greek yogurt

2 tbsp tahini paste

1 small garlic clove, crushed

1 tbsp freshly squeezed lemon juice

To serve

8 small ciabatta rolls

a handful of salad leaves

SERVES 4

In a bowl, combine the semi-dried tomatoes, preserved lemon, pine nuts, pomegranate seeds, parsley, 2 tablespoons of the oil, the honey and some salt and pepper. Set aside.

Cut the aubergine widthways into 8 thick slices. Combine 2 tablespoons of the remaining oil with the ras el hanout and some salt and pepper and brush over the slices.

Heat a ridged stove-top grill pan until hot and griddle the aubergine for 4–5 minutes on each side until well charred and softened.

Meanwhile, beat together the yogurt, tahini, garlic and lemon juice and season to taste.

To serve, cut the rolls in half and lightly toast the cut sides under the grill/broiler. Fill with the aubergine slices, tomato mixture, tahini sauce and salad leaves. Serve at once.

180 g/6 oz. lean minced/ground beef

3 tbsp breadcrumbs

½ red onion, finely chopped

2 tsp tomato purée/paste

20 g/3 tbsp grated Monterey Jack or sharp Cheddar cheese

freshly grated zest of ½ a lime

½ a fresh red chilli/chile, chopped

1 tbsp beaten egg

1 tbsp olive or vegetable oil

sea salt and freshly ground black pepper

Guacamole

1 large ripe avocado, peeled and pitted

½ fresh red chilli/chile, finely chopped

1 tsp lime juice

a handful of fresh coriander/cilantro

Tomato salsa

500 g/1 lb. 2 oz. ripe tomatoes, peeled and diced

½ a red onion, finely chopped

1–2 small green chillies/chiles, deseeded and finely chopped

3 tbsp lime juice

a pinch of sugar

2 tbsp finely chopped fresh coriander/ cilantro

To serve

2 large flour tortillas

sour cream

a handful of coriander/cilantro, chopped

SERVES 2

MEXICAN BURGER
WITH SOUR CREAM, SALSA & GUACAMOLE

This burger contains all the feisty flavours of Mexico as well as the accompaniments, so they power through with every bite. Add some extra chilli/chile if you like it hot.

To make the guacamole, put the avocado in a bowl with the chilli, lime juice, coriander and a pinch of sea salt and pepper, to taste. Mash together with a fork.

To make the tomato salsa, put the tomatoes in a bowl with the onion and chillies. Add the lime juice and mix well, then add the sugar and season with sea salt. Stir in the coriander/cilantro.

To make the burgers, put the beef in a bowl with the breadcrumbs, onion, tomato purée, cheese, lime zest, chilli, egg and a pinch of sea salt and pepper. Work together with your hands until evenly mixed. Divide the beef mixture in half and shape into two burger patties. Press each burger down to make them nice and flat.

Heat the oil in a frying pan/skillet and fry the burgers over medium–high heat for 5 minutes on each side until cooked through.

Preheat the grill/broiler to medium. Splash a few drops of water on each tortilla and lay them under the grill/broiler for a few seconds on each side to lightly toast. Spread both tortillas with sour cream and put a cooked burger on top of each. Top with a spoonful each of guacamole and tomato salsa. Sprinkle with coriander and serve, folding the sides of the tortilla around the burger to eat.

CHILAQUILE BURGER

A regular burger recipe goes from average to amazing with the addition of pepperoncini, tortilla chips and spicy arrabbiata sauce.

900 g/2 lb. minced/ground beef

750 ml/3 cups Arrabbiata Sauce (see recipe below)

30 g/2 tbsp butter

60 g/2 cups thick-cut plain tortilla chips

4 burger buns, split and toasted

4 slices of Cheddar cheese

170 g/1 cup jarred pickled Italian chilli peppers/ pepperoncini, chopped

salt and freshly ground black pepper

Arrabbiata sauce

1 tbsp vegetable oil

1 large onion, chopped

4 garlic cloves, crushed

2 x 400-g/14-oz. cans chopped tomatoes

2 tbsp tomato purée/paste

75 ml/⅓ cup white wine

1 tbsp white sugar

1 tsp chilli flakes/hot red pepper flakes, crushed

½ tsp Italian seasoning (optional)

1 tbsp each freshly chopped basil and flat-leaf parsley

SERVES 4

First, make the arrabbiata sauce. Add the vegetable oil to a large saucepan or pot set over medium heat. When the oil is hot, add the chopped onion and garlic. Sauté for 5 minutes, or until softened. Add the canned tomatoes, tomato purée, wine, sugar, chilli flakes and Italian seasoning (if using). Season well with salt and black pepper and bring to the boil. Reduce the heat to medium and simmer, uncovered, for about 15 minutes, stirring occasionally. Stir in the basil and parsley, check the seasoning and add more salt and pepper to taste. Use in the recipe below as directed. Any leftover sauce can be frozen for another time.

Form the beef into four thin 225-g/8-oz. patties. Set a ridged stove-top grill pan over medium-high heat. Season the burgers on one side with salt and pepper. When hot, add the burgers to the pan, seasoned-side down. Season the other side of the burger and cook to your liking.

In a medium frying pan/skillet, heat the arrabbiata sauce over medium heat. Add the butter and stir until it is melted. When the butter is melted, add the tortilla chips to the pan. Gently stir the pan to coat the chips while taking care not to break them. Set aside and keep warm.

Place a cooked burger on the bottom half of each burger bun, top with a slice of cheese, the tortilla mixture (chilaquiles) and the chopped pepperoncini before adding the top of the bun. Serve immediately.

JAMAICAN JERK TUNA BURGER WITH TABASCO MAYO

A triple whammy of heat in this burger with the jerk spice in the tuna, the avocado salsa and the Tabasco in the mayonnaise – if it isn't hot, it isn't Jamaican.

500 g/1 lb. 2 oz. fresh tuna steaks
grated zest and juice of 2 limes
2 spring onions/scallions, trimmed
   and chopped
1 garlic clove, crushed
50 g/1 cup soft white breadcrumbs
salt and freshly ground black pepper
olive oil, for frying

Jerk spice mix
1 tbsp allspice berries
1 tsp chilli flakes/hot red pepper flakes
2 tbsp soft brown sugar
1/2 tsp ground cinnamon
1/4 tsp ground cumin
1/4 tsp ground cloves

To serve
100 g/1/2 cup Classic Mayo
   (see page 112)
1 tsp Tabasco sauce
1 avocado
1 jalapeño chilli/chile, sliced
a handful of coriander/cilantro
   leaves
4 sesame bagels or buns
4 lettuce leaves

SERVES 2

Make the jerk spice mix. Place the allspice berries in a small frying pan/skillet and heat gently over medium heat for 1–2 minutes until they start to release their aroma. Allow to cool, then grind with the chilli flakes using a pestle and mortar or spice grinder. Combine with the sugar and ground spices. (Any spice mix not used in this recipe can be stored in a jar.)

Make the burgers. Dice the tuna and place in a food processor with 1 tablespoon of the jerk spice mix, the grated zest and juice of 1 lime, spring onions, garlic, breadcrumbs and a little salt and pepper. Using the pulse button, gradually blend the mixture until chopped but not mushy. Divide the mixture in half and shape into two burger patties. Press each burger down to make them nice and flat. Chill for 30 minutes.

Combine the Classic Mayo and Tabasco in a bowl. Peel and stone the avocado and thickly slice. Combine with the chilli, coriander leaves and the zest and juice of the remaining lime and season to taste.

Preheat a ridged stovetop grill pan over high heat. Brush the patties with a little oil and cook for 3 minutes on each side until charred. Rest for 5 minutes.

To serve, cut the bagels in half and toast the cut sides under the grill/broiler. Assemble the bagels with the lettuce leaves, tuna burgers, avocado salsa and Tabasco mayonnaise. Serve at once.

VIETNAMESE SESAME TOFU
BANH MI BURGER WITH PICKLED VEGETABLES

Here tofu is marinated in a char sui sauce, then grilled/broiled and served with pickled vegetables, chillies/chiles, salad leaves and fresh herbs, making this a delicious veggie alternative to the classic Vietnamese Barbecue pork rolls, or banh mi.

300 g/10½ oz. firm tofu
5 tbsp hoisin sauce
4 tbsp honey
4 tbsp dark soy sauce
2 tbsp Shaoxing wine
1 tsp sesame oil
1 tsp Chinese 5-spice powder

Pickled vegetables
1 small carrot
½ cucumber
½ small red onion
3½ tbsp rice wine vinegar
50 g/¼ cup caster/granulated sugar
1 tsp salt

To serve
1 French baguette
a handful of salad leaves
a few fresh coriander/cilantro,
   mint and basil leaves
4 tbsp Classic Mayo (see page 112)
4 tbsp sweet chilli/chile sauce
1 tbsp each black and white
   sesame seeds

SERVES 4

Make the pickled vegetables. Thinly slice the carrot lengthways, then cut into long thin strips. Deseed and cut the cucumber into long thin strips. Thinly slice the onion. Combine the vegetables in a bowl. Place the vinegar, sugar, 2 tablespoons water and salt in a saucepan and heat gently until the sugar has dissolved. Bring to the boil, then pour over the vegetables. Stir well and set aside to cool.

Cut the tofu into eight thick slices and place in a bowl. Combine the hoisin sauce, honey, soy sauce, Shaoxing wine, sesame oil and Chinese 5-spice powder. Pour over the tofu, turning to coat the slices thoroughly and leave to marinate for 30 minutes.

Heat a heavy-based frying pan/skillet over high heat and fry the marinated tofu slices in batches for 2 minutes on each side until charred.

To serve, cut the baguette into 10-cm/4-inch lengths, then slice each one almost in half horizontally. Fill each one with the salad leaves, fresh herbs, fried tofu and pickled vegetables and drizzle over the Classic Mayo and sweet chilli sauce. Scatter over the sesame seeds and serve at once.

CHAPTER 3

SLIDERS

450–680 g/1–1½ lb. extra lean minced/ground beef

2 spring onions/scallions, diced

1 tsp sea salt

1 tsp ground black pepper

½ tbsp olive oil

1 egg

Pickle relish

225 g/1 cup Sweet & Sour Cherry Pickles (see page 124), finely chopped

1 small white onion, chopped

3 garlic cloves, minced

1 tsp sugar

¼ tsp sea salt

Secret sauce

115 g/½ cup mayonnaise

2 tbsp creamy French dressing

3 tbsp Pickle Relish (see above)

½ small white onion, finely diced

1 tsp vinegar

1 tsp caster/granulated sugar

pinch of salt

To serve

8–12 slices of American or Cheddar cheese

8–12 slider buns

iceberg lettuce, cut into strips

Spicy Dill Pickles (see page 124), sliced

Sweet Potato Fries (see page 120)

MAKES 8–12

SLIDERS WITH SECRET SAUCE

Popularized in New York in the 1990s, this tasty mini-hamburger is in many ways the quintessential American burger.

Make the pickle relish in advance, by mixing all the ingredients in a bowl and storing in a jar or Tupperware container to marinate for at least 24 hours.

In a medium mixing bowl, combine the minced beef, diced onions, salt, pepper, olive oil and egg. Mix well with your hands and then press the meat mixture into patties. You can use a cookie cutter to get even and equal-sized sliders. This recipe makes 8–12 sliders depending on the size you prefer.

In a small bowl, combine the secret sauce ingredients and season to taste.

Cook the sliders on a grill or pan-fry them to your liking. Place a slice of cheese on top of the hot slider to let it melt a little. Meanwhile, cut the slider buns in half and spread the secret sauce on the bottom half. Chop the iceberg lettuce into strips and place a few on top of the sauce. Put the slider and cheese on top, followed by more secret sauce and a couple of sliced Spicy Dill Pickles. Add the top half of the bun.

Serve the sliders warm with Sweet Potato Fries and extra dill pickles.

16 large raw prawns/shrimp, peeled and deveined
1 tbsp sunflower oil
zest and juice of 1 lime
2 tsp caster/granulated sugar
2 tsp sea salt

Sambal

2 large shallots, chopped
2 Thai red chillies/chiles, seeded and chopped
2 large garlic cloves, sliced
½ tsp ground turmeric
1 tbsp peanut oil
2 tbsp coconut cream
1 tbsp tamarind paste
1 tbsp light soy sauce
2 tbsp white sugar
1 large tomato, diced
salt

To serve

8 mini brioche rolls
a handful of Asian salad leaves
4 tbsp Classic Mayo (see page 112)
a few coriander/cilantro leaves

16 bamboo skewers, soaked

SERVES 4

MALAYSIAN PRAWN SAMBAL SLIDERS

Malaysian sambals, or sauces, are a blend of Asian and Indian flavours, and it is the turmeric that gives this one its distinctive colour and taste. It's a delicious complement to the charred prawns/shrimp.

Make the sambal. Place the shallots, chillies, garlic, turmeric and a pinch of salt in a food processor with 1 tablespoon water and blend to a smooth paste. Heat the peanut oil in a small wok or frying pan/skillet and gently fry the paste for 5 minutes over very low heat until fragrant. Stir in the coconut cream, tamarind paste, soy sauce and sugar and cook, stirring, for 1 minute, then add the tomato. Simmer gently for 10 minutes until the sauce has thickened. Leave to cool.

Place the prawns in a shallow dish and combine with the sunflower oil, lime zest, sugar and salt. Thread the prawns lengthways onto the soaked bamboo skewers to keep them as flat as you can and leave to marinate for 15 minutes.

Heat a ridged stovetop grill pan over high heat and cook the prawns for 1–2 minutes on each side until charred and cooked through. Remove from the heat and dress with the lime juice. Rest for 3 minutes.

To serve, cut the rolls in half and lightly toast the cut sides under a grill/broiler. Fill with salad leaves, sambal, prawns, Classic Mayo and coriander. Serve at once.

BEEF & MOZZARELLA SLIDERS
WITH PESTO MAYO

These simple beef sliders have a delightfully gooey mozzarella surprise in the middle – great for a party or as part of a buffet.

200 g/7 oz. lean minced/
   ground beef
2 tsp tomato purée/paste
1 garlic clove, finely chopped
4 mozzarella pearls/bocconcini
a pinch of sea salt and freshly
   ground black pepper

To serve
4 mini ciabattas
Pesto Mayo (see page 113)
a handful of rocket/arugula leaves

MAKES 4 SLIDERS

Preheat the oven to 180°C (350°F) Gas 4.

Put the beef in a bowl with the tomato purée, garlic and salt and pepper. Work together with your hands until evenly mixed. Divide the beef mixture into quarters and shape into four slider patties. Put a mozzarella pearl in the middle of each and then fold the beef mixture around it to reform the slider patties, with the mozzarella pearl hidden in the middle. Press each slider down to make them nice and flat.

Lay the sliders on a baking sheet and bake in the preheated oven for 20 minutes, turning halfway through cooking. When cooked, remove from the oven and let stand for 4 minutes before serving to allow the mozzarella to cool a little.

Slice the mini ciabattas in half and spread the bottom half of each with a little Pesto Mayo. Put a cooked slider on top and add a few rocket leaves. Finish the sliders with the lids of the mini ciabattas and serve.

1 tbsp canned black beans
1 spring onion/scallion, sliced
1 garlic clove, finely chopped
2 tsp tomato purée/paste
a pinch of cayenne pepper
1 tbsp chopped fresh coriander/
    cilantro
200 g/7 oz. lean minced/ground beef
40 g/3 tbsp long-grain rice, cooked
    and cooled
1 tbsp olive or vegetable oil
sea salt and freshly ground
    black pepper

Corn & pepper salsa

2 large corn cobs
3 tbsp vegetable oil
4 spring onions/scallions, sliced
freshly squeezed juice of 1 lime
6 Pepperdew peppers, diced
2 tbsp finely chopped coriander/
    cilantro
a dash of chilli/chili sauce

To serve

4 mini poppyseed rolls
Lime Mayo (see page 113)
Sweet Potato Fries (see page 120)

MAKES 4 SLIDERS

BEEF & BLACK BEAN SLIDERS
WITH CORN & PEPPER SALSA

These delicious beef sliders, served with a spicy salsa and tangy mayo are guaranteed to create a fiesta of flavours.

To make the corn and pepper salsa, cut down the sides of the corn cobs with a sharp knife to remove the kernels. Heat 2 teaspoons of the oil in a frying pan/skillet set over medium heat. Add the corn and cook for 2–3 minutes until it begins to brown. Add the spring onions and cook for 1 minute. Transfer to a bowl and let cool.

Add the lime juice, peppers, coriander and the remaining oil, and mix. Add the chilli sauce and season with salt and pepper.

To make the sliders, blitz the black beans, spring onion, garlic, tomato purée, cayenne pepper and coriander in a food processor. Pour the mixture into a mixing bowl, add the beef and work together with your hands until evenly mixed. Add the cooled rice, season with salt and pepper and mix again.

Divide the beef mixture into quarters and shape into four slider patties. Press each slider down to make them nice and flat.

Heat the oil in a frying pan and fry the sliders over medium–high heat for 4 minutes on each side until cooked through.

Slice the mini poppyseed rolls in half and spread the bottom half of each with Lime Mayo. Put a cooked slider on top of each and add a large spoonful of Corn and Pepper Salsa. Finish the sliders with the lids of the rolls and serve with Sweet Potato Fries on the side, if liked.

JAPANESE SALMON KATSU SLIDERS

Small salmon patties coated in breadcrumbs and served with a katsu sauce make really tasty fish sliders. Add some wasabi for optional heat!

1 tsp sunflower oil,
  plus 1 tbsp for frying
1 tsp sesame oil
2 shallots, finely chopped
1 tsp grated fresh ginger
400 g/14 oz. skinless salmon fillets
2 tsp miso paste
50 g/1 cup panko breadcrumbs
salt and freshly ground
  black pepper

Katsu sauce
4 tbsp tomato ketchup
2 tbsp Worcestershire sauce
2 tbsp oyster sauce
4 tsp caster/granulated sugar

To serve
8 mixed mini rolls
a handful of salad leaves
3 tbsp pickled ginger
a little wasabi paste (optional)

SERVES 4

Heat 1 teaspoon sunflower oil and the sesame oil in a frying pan/skillet and gently fry the shallots and ginger for 5 minutes until soft. Let cool.

Combine 300 g/10½ oz. of the salmon with the shallot mixture, miso paste and a little salt and pepper and purée in a food processor until fairly smooth. Finely dice the remaining salmon and stir through the minced mixture. Shape the mixture into eight small patties, pressing each one down to make them nice and flat, and chill for 30 minutes.

Preheat the oven to 190°C (375°F) Gas 5 and line a baking sheet with baking parchment.

Meanwhile, make the katsu sauce. Combine all the ingredients in a bowl, stirring to dissolve the sugar. Set aside.

Place the breadcrumbs in a shallow bowl and dip in the patties, pressing the crumbs over the surface to coat them completely.

Heat 1 tablespoon sunflower oil in a large frying pan/skillet and cook the patties for 1 minute on each side over medium heat. Transfer to the prepared baking sheet and bake in the preheated oven for 5–10 minutes, or until cooked through. Remove from the oven and rest for 5 minutes.

To serve, cut the rolls in half and lightly toast the cut sides under the grill/broiler. Fill each roll with a burger, salad leaves, pickled ginger, wasabi (if using) and katsu sauce. Serve at once.

100 g/3½ oz. lean minced/
ground beef

100 g/3½ oz. lean minced/
ground pork

1 fresh red or green chilli/chile,
finely chopped

1 tbsp freshly squeezed
lime juice

½ tsp ground ginger

3 tbsp fresh breadcrumbs

1 tbsp olive or vegetable oil

a pinch of sea salt and freshly
ground black pepper

To serve

6 chicory/Belgian endive leaves

2 fresh red chillies/chiles, deseeded
and finely sliced

2 spring onions/scallions,
finely sliced

6 cocktail sticks/toothpicks
(optional)

MAKES 6 SLIDERS

SPICY BEEF & PORK SLIDERS WITH GINGER & LIME

These punchy Asian-style sliders are ideal for eating outdoors on a warm summer's evening. The lime and ginger soak perfectly into the meat and a touch of spice adds a welcome kick to every mouthful.

Put the beef and pork in a bowl with the chilli, lime juice, ginger, breadcrumbs and salt and pepper. Work together with your hands until evenly mixed. Divide the beef mixture into six equal pieces and shape into six slider patties. Press each slider down to make them nice and flat.

Heat the oil in a frying pan/skillet and fry the sliders over medium-high heat for 3 minutes on each side until cooked through.

Put the chicory leaves face up on a serving plate. Put a slider on top of each leaf and top with chilli and spring onions. Put a cocktail stick through the middle of each slider to hold them together, if liked, and serve.

INDIAN-STYLE LAMB SLIDERS
WITH MINTED YOGURT & MANGO CHUTNEY

*These deliciously spiced Indian-style sliders pack a good punch.
Served on mini naan breads, they look great and are perfect canapés
for a party or appetizers for an Indian-style feast.*

200 g/7 oz. lean minced/
  ground lamb

1 tbsp garam masala

a pinch of ground turmeric

3 tbsp fresh breadcrumbs

1 tbsp beaten egg

a pinch of chopped fresh
  coriander/cilantro

1 tbsp olive oil, for frying

a pinch of sea salt and freshly
  ground black pepper

To serve

4 mini naan breads

plain yogurt mixed with freshly
  chopped mint leaves

mango chutney

*cocktail sticks/toothpicks
  (optional)*

MAKES 4 SLIDERS

Put the lamb in a bowl with the garam masala, turmeric,
breadcrumbs, egg, coriander and salt and pepper. Divide
the mixture into quarters and shape into 4 slider patties.
Press each slider down to make them nice and flat.

Heat the oil in a frying pan/skillet and fry the sliders over
medium-high heat for 4 minutes on each side until cooked.

Splash a little water on each of the mini naan breads and
toast under the grill/broiler or in a toaster to warm. Put a
generous spoonful of minted yogurt over the top of each
mini naan. Top with a cooked slider and finish with a
spoonful of mango chutney. Put a cocktail stick through
the middle of each, if needed, and serve.

CHINESE CRISPY DUCK SLIDERS
WITH HOISIN & SPRING ONIONS/SCALLIONS

*These duck burgers are lovely with the brioche rolls as an alternative to
Chinese steamed buns; you could also substitute with bao buns if preferred.*

2 x 450 g/1 lb. duck leg confit,
   at room temperature
2 tbsp honey
2 tbsp soy sauce
2 tsp hoisin sauce, plus extra
   to serve
1 tsp Chinese 5-spice powder
50 g/⅓ cup plain/all-purpose flour
2 eggs, beaten
75 g/1 cup dried breadcrumbs
sunflower oil, for frying
salt and freshly ground black pepper

To serve
8 oval or round brioche rolls
4 spring onions/scallions,
   trimmed and cut into strips
1 small cucumber, deseeded and
   cut into thin batons

*a roasting pan, lined with
   baking parchment*

MAKES 8

Set 1 tablespoon of fat from the duck confit aside and reserve.
Discard the remaining fat. Place the duck in the roasting pan.

Combine the honey, soy sauce and hoisin sauce in a bowl
and add a pinch of salt. Brush all over the duck legs and roast
in the preheated oven for 15 minutes, brushing with the glaze
in the pan halfway through until golden. Let cool.

Roughly tear the duck skin and flesh into small pieces and
place in a food processor with the reserved fat and the
Chinese 5-spice powder and a little salt and pepper. Pulse
briefly until the mixture just comes together.

Divide the duck mixture into eight small slider patties and press
each slider down to make them nice and flat. Dip each one into
the flour, then the beaten egg and finally the breadcrumbs,
turning over until coated with crumbs. Chill for 30 minutes.

Preheat the oven to 190°C (375°F) Gas 5.

Heat about 1 tablespoon sunflower oil in a large frying pan/
skillet and fry the patties in batches for 2 minutes on each side
until golden. Transfer to a clean baking sheet and bake for a
further 5 minutes until cooked through.

To serve, cut the brioche rolls in half and lightly toast the cut
sides under the grill/broiler. Fill with the duck sliders, spring
onions, cucumber and some extra hoisin sauce. Serve at once.

CHICKEN CAESAR SLIDERS
WRAPPED IN PARMA HAM WITH CAESAR DRESSING

These cute sliders combine all the ingredients of a chicken Caesar salad. They're light and delicious and make great canapés to serve at parties – perfect for entertaining.

200 g/7 oz. lean minced/ground chicken or turkey
6 chives, finely chopped
1 tsp anchovy paste
20 g/¾ oz. Parmesan cheese, finely grated
1 tsp beaten egg
a pinch of sea salt and freshly ground black pepper
2 slices of Parma ham, cut in half

Caesar dressing
1 egg yolk
1 small garlic clove, crushed
2 anchovy fillets in oil, drained and chopped
1 tbsp freshly squeezed lemon juice
1 tsp Worcestershire sauce
150 ml/⅔ cup olive oil
25 g/1 oz. Parmesan cheese, finely grated
sea salt and freshly ground black pepper

To serve
4 seeded mini rolls
a handful of Romano lettuce leaves

4 cocktail sticks/toothpicks

MAKES 4 SLIDERS

Preheat the oven to 180°C (350°F) Gas 4.

To make the Caesar dressing, whisk the egg yolk in a small bowl with the garlic, anchovies, lemon juice, Worcestershire sauce and salt and pepper, to taste, until frothy. Gradually whisk in the olive oil a little at a time until thick and glossy. Add 2 tablespoons of water to thin the dressing and stir in the Parmesan. Store in a screw-top jar in the fridge and use the same day.

To make the sliders, put the chicken in a bowl with the chives, anchovy paste, Parmesan, egg and salt and pepper. Work together with your hands until evenly mixed. Divide the mixture into quarters and shape into four slider patties. Press each slider down to make them nice and flat.

Wrap a piece of Parma ham around each slider and lay them on a baking sheet. Bake the sliders in the preheated oven for 15–20 minutes until cooked through.

Cut each of the rolls in half and put a Romano lettuce leaf on the bottom half of each roll. Top each with a cooked slider, drizzle with Caesar dressing and finish with the lids of the rolls. Put a cocktail stick/toothpick through the middle of each slider to hold it in place and serve.

CHAPTER 4

**VEGGIE
& VEGAN**

CHUNKY HUMMUS BURGERS

The beetroot/beet in this recipe turns the burgers bright pink, which in turn makes them very popular with kids! However, you could replace the beetroot with another root vegetable if you prefer.

80 g/½ cup couscous

125 ml/½ cup boiling water

200 g/1 cup hummus, ideally homemade

50 g/¼ cup finely grated vegetables (beetroots/beets, carrots, parsnip, celeriac/celery root, etc.)

40 g/1 small onion, finely chopped

2 garlic cloves, finely chopped

½ tsp dried oregano

2 tbsp finely chopped parsley or finely snipped chives

sea salt and freshly ground black pepper

To serve

burger buns

vegan mayonnaise

lettuce

sliced gherkins

red onions

baking sheets lined with baking parchment

MAKES 6 BURGERS

Preheat the oven to 180°C (350°F) Gas 4.

Place the couscous in a bowl, pour over the boiling water, cover and let sit for 5 minutes.

Place all the ingredients in a mixing bowl and knead into a well-combined dough. Divide the mixture into 6 portions and form them into even burgers with your hands. Place them on the lined baking sheet.

Bake in the preheated oven for 20–25 minutes, or until a nice crust forms and the burgers start browning lightly. Here, these are served in a bun with vegan mayonnaise, lettuce, gherkins and red onion. But the trimmings are really up to you!

BLACK BEAN BURGER

Black beans make for a tasty alternative to traditional beef burgers, and the addition of corn kernels brings texture and sweetness. They are a bit on the delicate side, so take care to turn them carefully as they cook.

2 onions, diced

a splash of olive oil, for frying

3 garlic cloves, chopped

400-g/14-oz. can black beans, drained and rinsed

200-g/7-oz. can sweetcorn/ corn kernels, drained

½ x 400-g/14-oz. can black beluga lentils, drained and rinsed

2 tbsp smoked paprika

25 g/¼ cup porridge/rolled oats

1 tbsp plain/all-purpose flour

a few sprigs of fresh coriander/ cilantro, chopped

salt and freshly ground black pepper

4 burger-cheese slices (optional)

To serve

4 burger buns, sliced in half (I like the brioche ones)

tomato ketchup

2 vine tomatoes, sliced

½ iceberg lettuce, shredded

mayonnaise

SERVES 4

Fry the onions in a splash of olive oil in a frying pan/skillet over low heat for about 10 minutes, then add the garlic and warm through for another couple of minutes, then remove from the heat.

Tip the beans into a large mixing bowl, mash with the back of a fork until well puréed, or as best as you can do. Tip the sweetcorn onto a chopping board and run a knife over them, just to break them up slightly, then add to the bowl of beans along with the lentils, smoked paprika, oats, flour, coriander and cooked onions and garlic. Season very generously with salt and black pepper.

Heat a heavy-based frying pan and drizzle in a splash of olive oil. Form 4 patties with the burger mixture and place them into the pan – don't move them. Leave them to char on the outside for a few minutes before carefully turning them over. Don't worry if they break up a little. As soon as you've turned them, lay a cheese slice on top (if using) and continue cooking for a few more minutes.

Finally, toast the burger buns in a ridged stovetop grill pan or in a lightly oiled frying pan, lace with ketchup, place a burger patty on top, followed by a couple of slices of tomato, some lettuce, then mayo and finish with the top of the bun.

SPICY VEGAN RICE & VEGGIE BURGERS

Making a good vegan burger is a tricky business, but this recipe is a winner.
These baked sweet potato wedges are a nice alternative to fries as a side.

80 g/³⁄₄ cup vegetable pulp or
    grated vegetables (use anything
    that needs using up in the fridge
    – carrots, sweet potatoes,
    courgette/zucchini all work well)
50 g/¹⁄₃ cup finely diced onion
3 garlic cloves, crushed
1 tsp barbecue spice mix
¹⁄₄ tsp sweet paprika
¹⁄₄ tsp ground turmeric
¹⁄₈ tsp chilli/chili powder
4 tbsp finely chopped fresh herbs
    (parsley, chives, etc.)
575 g/3¹⁄₃ cups cooked brown rice,
    room temperature
³⁄₄ tsp sea salt
plain/all-purpose flour, for coating
sunflower oil, for frying

To serve
your favourite pickles
    (see page 124)
red onion slices
vegan mayonnaise
Sweet Potato Fries (see page 120)

*baking sheet lined with foil and
    roasting rack placed on top*

SERVES 4–5

For the burgers, put all the ingredients (except the flour and
the oil) in a big bowl. Using your hands, knead the mixture
until everything is combined and the rice starts becoming
sticky. This will prevent the burgers from falling apart or
absorbing too much oil. Taste and add more salt and spice
if needed. Allow the mixture to rest for 30 minutes.

With moist hands, start shaping the mixture into small, neat
burgers – you should be able to make about 14. Roll each
burger in a little flour and set aside.

Meanwhile, fill a deep, heavy-bottomed frying pan/skillet
with 3 cm/1¼ inches vegetable oil and heat it until the oil starts
moving. Throw a small piece of the mixture into the pan: if it
starts sizzling, it's ready to go. Deep-fry a couple of burgers at
a time without overcrowding, depending on the size of your
pan. When they turn golden brown, remove them from the
oil with a slotted spoon and place them on paper towels.
They should be golden with a thin crust and a juicy inside.

Serve the burgers hot with the pickles, onion slices,
mayonnaise and Sweet Potato Fries. Enjoy!

INDIAN-SPICED CAULI BURGERS

These open cauli burgers served on naan bread make a great alternative to a classic burger. You can freeze some of the burgers for another time if needed.

200 g/7 oz. quinoa
1 head of cauliflower
3–4 tbsp olive oil
1 tsp ground cumin
1 tsp ground coriander
1 tsp chilli/chili powder (optional)
2 garlic cloves, crushed
100 g/1¼ cups dried breadcrumbs
50 g/½ cup ground almonds
100 g/1 cup grated paneer
3 eggs
2 green chillies/chiles, finely chopped
handful of coriander/cilantro, finely chopped
salt and freshly ground black pepper

To serve

small round naan breads
raita
mango chutney
spring onions/scallions, thinly sliced
lettuce leaves
coriander/cilantro
shaved cucumber ribbons
lime wedges, for squeezing

baking sheet, lined

MAKES 10

Preheat the oven to 200°C (400°F) Gas 6.

Cook the quinoa according to the package instructions. Drain, leave to cool in the sieve/strainer and pat dry with paper towels to remove as much moisture as possible.

Cut the cauliflower into florets, transfer to a baking sheet, drizzle with 1 tablespoon of the oil and sprinkle with the spices. Roast in the preheated oven for 20–30 minutes, then leave to cool. Pulse in a food processor to roughly chop into small pieces that stick together.

Combine the cooked, pulsed cauliflower with the quinoa, garlic, breadcrumbs, ground almonds, paneer, eggs, green chillies, coriander and some salt and pepper.

Divide the mixture into 10 portions, then shape each one into a small patty/burger.

Place the burgers on the lined baking sheet and bake in the preheated oven for 25–30 minutes until golden. Serve each burger on a naan bread, with some raita, mango chutney, spring onions, lettuce leaves, coriander, shaved cucumber ribbons and a squeeze of lime.

3 tbsp olive oil

1 onion, finely chopped

2 garlic cloves, crushed

75 g/½ cup black beans

120 g/1 cup cooked quinoa

100 g/½ cup cooked sweet potato, flesh scooped out

1 carrot, shredded

½ tsp ground cumin

½ tsp ground coriander

2 tbsp parsley, chopped

15 g/⅛ cup breadcrumbs

5 portobello mushrooms

a pinch each of sea salt and freshly ground black pepper

To serve

1 avocado, peeled, pitted and sliced

1 large tomato, sliced

1 gherkin/pickle, chopped

½ red onion, sliced

a handful of fresh coriander/ cilantro

1–2 tbsp freshly squeezed lime juice

a baking sheet lined with baking parchment

MAKES 5 BURGERS

QUINOA BURGERS
WITH PORTOBELLO MUSHROOMS

Nutritious quinoa mixes with sweet potato and black beans to give these burgers a satisfying texture.

Preheat the oven to 180°C (350°F) Gas 4.

Heat 1 tablespoon of the olive oil in a saucepan over medium heat. Fry the onions for about 3 minutes until softened. Add the garlic and cook for another minute. Add the beans, stir and cook for a few minutes longer. Remove from the heat and transfer the mixture to a large mixing bowl.

Lightly mash the beans with a fork until they're semi-crushed. Add the rest of the ingredients (except the mushrooms and remaining olive oil) and mix well. If the mixture is too moist, add extra breadcrumbs. If too dry, add some more beans.

Form the mixture into patties with your hands and place on the prepared baking sheet. Bake in the preheated oven for 20–25 minutes, checking after about 15 minutes and turning to ensure even browning. Once cooked, remove from the oven and cover to keep warm.

Increase the temperature of the oven to 200°C (400°F) Gas 6.

For the mushroom base, clean the mushrooms with a damp cloth. Remove the stems and drizzle with the remaining olive oil. Season with salt and pepper and roast for 20 minutes.

When ready to serve, place each burger on top of a roasted mushroom and garnish with your choice of burger toppings.

BUFFALO CAULIFLOWER BURGER
WITH BLUE CHEESE SAUCE

A classic American chicken wing dish is here given the veggie treatment, with roast cauliflower florets replacing the chicken.

75 g/½ cup chickpea/gram flour
  or plain/all-purpose flour
1 tsp mustard powder
1 tsp ground cumin
1 tsp smoked paprika
120 ml/½ cup whole milk
florets from 1 cauliflower,
  about 500 g/1 lb. 2 oz.
2 tbsp chilli/chile sauce
1 tbsp clear honey
1 tbsp butter
salt and freshly ground black pepper

Blue cheese dressing
4 tbsp sour cream
50 g/2 oz. creamy blue cheese
1 tbsp white wine vinegar
1 tbsp freshly chopped chives
½ tsp caster/granulated sugar
salt and freshly ground black pepper

To serve
4 burger buns
6–8 leaves of iceberg lettuce

SERVES 4

Preheat the oven to 220°C (425°F) Gas 7 and line a baking sheet with baking parchment.

In a bowl, combine the flour, mustard powder, cumin, paprika and a little salt and pepper. Gradually whisk in the milk with 50 ml/3½ tablespoons cold water until the batter is smooth.

Dip each cauliflower floret into the batter and then shake off the excess so the cauliflower is just very lightly coated. Place on the prepared baking sheet, leaving space in between each floret. Roast in the preheated oven for 20 minutes.

Warm together the chilli sauce, honey and butter in a small saucepan over low heat until combined. Remove the cauliflower from the oven, drizzle over the warm sauce and stir well until evenly coated. Return to the oven for a further 10-15 minutes until the cauliflower is tender and golden. Let cool for 10 minutes.

Meanwhile, make the blue cheese dressing. Place the sour cream, blue cheese, vinegar and a little salt and pepper in a blender and whizz until fairly smooth. Stir in the chives and sugar; adjust seasoning to taste.

To serve, cut the buns in half and toast the cut sides under the grill/broiler. Fill with the lettuce, top with the cauliflower and drizzle over the blue cheese dressing. Serve at once.

CHILLI VEGGIE BURGER WITH SUN-DRIED TOMATOES

These deliciously savoury burgers are just spicy enough, with wonderful sweet hints from the sun-dried tomatoes and the polenta/cornmeal giving them a lovely crunch.

1 sweet potato, peeled and chopped into 2.5-cm/1-inch cubes

3 garlic cloves, skins on

olive oil, for drizzling

40 g/3 tbsp Puy lentils (or other green lentils)

1 tsp vegetable bouillon powder

60 g/½ cup fresh wholemeal/wholewheat breadcrumbs

1 carrot, grated

6–8 sun-dried tomatoes, finely chopped

1 medium–hot red chilli/chile, deseeded and finely chopped

1 tsp balsamic vinegar

1 tsp dried oregano

1 tsp dark soy sauce

1 tsp Cajun spice blend

1 small egg, lightly beaten

1 tbsp plain/all-purpose flour

1 tbsp polenta/cornmeal

celery salt and freshly ground black pepper

To serve

8 burger buns, warmed

rocket/arugula leaves

red onion relish or condiment of your choice

MAKES 8 BURGERS

Preheat the oven to 160°C (325°F) Gas 3.

Put the sweet potato in a roasting dish with the garlic and drizzle with olive oil. Roast for 40 minutes, or until the potato is soft and just beginning to colour. Leave to cool slightly.

Meanwhile, place the lentils in a pan of cold water with the vegetable bouillon, bring to the boil, then reduce the heat to a simmer and cook for 20–25 minutes until tender. Once the lentils are ready, drain them and place in a large mixing bowl. Add the breadcrumbs, carrot, sun-dried tomatoes, chilli, vinegar, oregano, soy sauce and Cajun spice blend.

Add the cooled sweet potato. Make sure the garlic is cool too, then squeeze it out from its skin into the mix. Use your hands to combine all the ingredients together. Season with celery salt and pepper. Add the egg to the mix to bind everything together. If the burger mix is too wet, add another handful of breadcrumbs to it.

Mix the flour and polenta together in a shallow bowl. Form the burger mix into 8 equal balls, roll in the flour mix and shape into a burger patty. Cover with cling film/plastic wrap until ready to cook.

Heat a little olive oil in a frying pan/skillet and fry the burgers over medium heat for about 5 minutes each side, turning frequently. Swerve in warm buns with rocket and spicy red onion relish.

CURRIED SWEET POTATO BURGERS

You can either add some lime pickle and natural yogurt to these nutty burgers, or serve them rolled in warm chapatti bread. Bulghur is a cracked wheat and is available from supermarkets and health food shops.

75 g/1½ cup bulghur wheat

400 g/14 oz. sweet potatoes, peeled and cubed

1½ tbsp olive oil, plus extra for shallow frying

1 small onion, finely chopped

1 garlic clove, crushed

1 tbsp curry powder

75 g/½ cup blanched almonds, finely chopped

2 tbsp chopped fresh coriander/cilantro

1 egg, lightly beaten

4 tbsp chickpea flour or plain/all-purpose flour

sea salt and freshly ground black pepper

To serve

4 burger buns/herbed rolls/chapatti bread

a handful of salad leaves

sliced cucumber

4 tbsp mango chutney

lime pickle

plain yogurt

SERVES 4

Put the bulghur wheat in a heatproof bowl, add boiling water to cover by 3 cm/1 inch and set aside to soak for about 20 minutes until tender. Drain well.

Meanwhile, steam the sweet potatoes for 10–15 minutes until cooked. Drain well and mash with a potato masher.

Heat the olive oil in a frying pan/skillet and fry the onion, garlic and curry powder for about 10 minutes until the onion is softened.

Put the bulghur wheat, mashed sweet potato, onion mixture, almonds, coriander, egg, flour and some salt and pepper in a bowl. Work together with your hands until evenly mixed. Cover and chill for 30 minutes. Using wet hands, divide the mixture into eight portions and shape into burger patties. Press each burger down to make them nice and flat.

Heat a shallow layer of olive oil in a frying pan/skillet, add the patties and fry gently for 3–4 minutes on each side until golden and heated through. Lightly toast the buns under the grill/broiler and fill with the patties, salad leaves, cucumber slices and mango chutney. Top with some lime pickle and yogurt, if using, and serve at once.

MUSHROOM BURGERS

Creamy Camembert cheese pairs well with mushrooms in this flavourful, vegetarian take on a classic hamburger.

2 tbsp olive oil

1 large red onion, halved and thinly sliced

2 fresh thyme sprigs

¼ tsp white sugar

1 tsp balsamic vinegar

2 tsp butter

2 large, flat mushrooms, stalks removed

salt and freshly ground black pepper

To serve

burger buns, halved

mayonnaise

iceberg lettuce

thin slices of Camembert

SERVES 2

Heat 1 tablespoon of the olive oil in a large, heavy frying pan/skillet. Add the red onion and thyme and fry gently over low heat for 8 minutes, stirring now and then, until softened. Add the sugar and vinegar and fry for 2 minutes more until caramelized. Set aside.

Wipe the frying pan/skillet clean. Heat the remaining olive oil and the butter over medium heat. Add the mushrooms and fry for 5 minutes, turning often, until browned on both sides. Season with salt and freshly ground black pepper.

Briefly grill/broil the burger buns, cut-side up, until just golden. Spread the bottom half with mayonnaise. Layer lettuce, a mushroom, Camembert cheese and half the caramelized onions in each bun. Serve at once.

BLACK BEAN & BEETROOT BURGERS

This smoky veggie burger works well with lots of different flavours,
so don't skimp on the toppings to create your favourite combinations.

olive oil, for frying
1 small red onion, finely diced
2 garlic cloves, finely chopped
2 tbsp flax seeds
50 g/½ cup porridge/rolled oats
2 x 400-g/14-oz. cans black beans,
  drained and rinsed
2 medium beetroot/beets, grated
2 tbsp tomato purée/paste
1½ tsp smoked paprika
1 tsp dried oregano
salt and freshly ground
  black pepper, to taste

To serve
toasted English muffins or buns
barbecue sauce
smashed avocado
caramelized or crispy onions
sliced tomato
Cos/romaine lettuce or rocket/
  arugula

MAKES 6–8 PATTIES

Heat a thin layer of olive oil in a medium frying pan/skillet over medium heat. Add the onion and cook, stirring, for about 5 minutes until softened. Add the garlic and cook for 1 minute more. Remove from the heat and set aside.

In a large bowl, combine the flax seeds with 6 tablespoons water and let stand for 10 minutes.

Meanwhile, in a food processor, process the oats until they are finely chopped and bordering on a flour-like texture. Add the black beans to the food processor and pulse until they're finely chopped and combined with the oats, but not puréed.

Add the processed oats and black beans, beetroot, onions and garlic, tomato purée, paprika and oregano to the flax seeds. Season with salt and pepper and mix with a rubber spatula or with your hands until well combined. Form the mixture into 6–8 patties using damp hands, making them about 2.5 cm/1 inch thick and about 7.5 cm/3–4 inches wide.

In a large frying pan/skillet, heat enough oil to cover the base over medium-high heat. Add two patties and cook for 3–4 minutes on one side, until browned and firm. Flip and cook for another 3–4 minutes on the other side. Reduce the heat to medium if the patties are getting too charred. Remove and repeat with the remaining burgers.

Serve warm on toasted English muffins or buns with plenty of your chosen toppings.

CHAPTER 5

SAUCES & SIDES

SAUCES

These sauces taste fantastic, are simple to make and will complement your burger and fries beautifully, giving plenty of chances for dipping.

TOMATO KETCHUP

1 kg/2 lb. 3 oz. tomatoes, cored and chopped
150 ml/⅔ cup vinegar (malt or cider)
50 g/¼ cup soft dark brown sugar

½ tsp fine salt
pinch of ground cinnamon
pinch of ground cloves
pinch of celery salt

MAKES ABOUT 400 ML/1¾ CUPS

Put the tomatoes in a saucepan and cook over medium-high heat, stirring occasionally, until they break down, 15–20 minutes. Transfer to a food processor and whizz until smooth, then rub through a fine-mesh sieve/strainer and return the paste to a clean pan. Continue cooking the tomato pulp over low heat, stirring often, until very thick. Stir in the remaining ingredients and simmer for 5 minutes. Taste and adjust seasoning, adding more vinegar and/or sugar according to taste. The sauce will keep, covered, in the fridge for at least 1 week.

CURRY KETCHUP

1 small onion, grated
2 tbsp vegetable oil
2 tbsp curry powder
1 tbsp hot paprika
1/2 tsp mustard powder
pinch of ground cloves
500 g/1 lb. 2 oz. passata/strained
   tomatoes
6 tbsp dark brown sugar
125 ml/1/2 cup malt vinegar
salt

MAKES ABOUT 400 ML/1¾ CUPS

In a saucepan, soften the onion
in the oil, 3–5 minutes. Stir in all
the spices and cook until aromatic,
about 1 minute more. Add the passata,
sugar, vinegar and salt to taste. Stir
to dissolve and bring to the boil,
then lower the heat and simmer
until thick like ketchup. Taste and
adjust seasoning. The sauce will
keep, covered, in the fridge for at
least 1 week.

CHILLI KETCHUP

1 small onion, finely chopped
1 tbsp vegetable oil
1 garlic clove, crushed
700 g/1½ lb. passata/
   strained tomatoes
1/4 tsp chilli/hot
   red pepper flakes
1 tsp tomato ketchup
splash of cider vinegar
salt and freshly ground
   black pepper

MAKES ABOUT 500 ML/2 CUPS

In a saucepan, soften the onion
in the oil, 3–5 minutes. Stir in the
garlic, passata, chilli flakes and
ketchup and bring to the boil, then
lower the heat and simmer until
thick. Add some salt, pepper and a
splash of vinegar; taste and adjust
seasoning. It will keep, covered,
in the fridge for at least 1 week.

MAYOS

Homemade mayonnaise is far more tasty than storebought versions, and using a food processor means it's so simple to make.

CLASSIC MAYO

3 egg yolks
2 tsp Dijon mustard
2 tsp white wine vinegar or freshly squeezed lemon juice
½ tsp sea salt
300 ml/1¼ cups olive oil

MAKES ABOUT 400 ML/1¾ CUPS

Put the egg yolks, mustard, vinegar or lemon juice and salt in a food processor and blend until foaming. With the blade running, gradually pour in the oil through a funnel until thick and glossy. If it is too thick add a little water. Taste and adjust the seasoning, if necessary. Spoon into a bowl and serve. Keep in the fridge for up to three days.

MUSTARD MAYO

1 recipe Classic Mayo (see left)
2 tbsp wholegrain mustard

MAKES ABOUT 400 ML/1¾ CUPS

Make the Classic Mayo following the method in the recipe, left, but omitting the Dijon mustard. Transfer to a bowl and stir in the wholegrain mustard. Use as required or store as before.

HERB MAYO

1 recipe Classic Mayo (see left)
a handful of any fresh green
    herbs, such as basil, parsley
    or tarragon, chopped

**MAKES ABOUT
400 ML/1¾ CUPS**

Make the Classic Mayo
following the method in
the recipe, far left. Add the
herbs to the food processor
and blend until the sauce
is speckled green. Use as
required or store as before.

LEMON MAYO

1 recipe Classic Mayo (see left)
1 tsp freshly squeezed
    lemon juice
1 tsp finely grated lemon zest
a pinch of freshly ground
    black pepper

**MAKES ABOUT
400 ML/1¾ CUPS**

Make the Classic Mayo following
the method in the recipe, far left,
adding the lemon juice, zest and
pepper with the mustard and
vinegar. Blend until thickened.
Use as required or store as before.

Variation: For a Lime Mayo,
simply replace the lemon
zest and juice with
the zest and juice
from a lime.

PESTO MAYO

1 recipe Classic Mayo (see left)
1 tsp fresh green pesto

**MAKES ABOUT
400 ML/1¾ CUPS**

Make the Classic Mayo
following the method in the
recipe, far left, adding the
pesto at the same time as the
mustard and vinegar. Blend
until thickened. Use as
required or store as before.

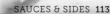

HOT & SMOKY BARBECUE SAUCE

200 ml/¾ cup passata/Italian
   sieved tomatoes

100 ml/scant ½ cup maple syrup

50 ml/3 tbsp black treacle/dark
   molasses

50 ml/3 tbsp Tomato Ketchup,
   homemade (see page 110)
   or store-bought

50 ml/3 tbsp white wine vinegar

2 tbsp Worcestershire sauce

1 tbsp hot chilli/chili sauce

2 tsp Dijon mustard

1 tsp garlic powder

1 tsp smoked paprika

sea salt and freshly ground
   black pepper

MAKES 350 ML/1½ CUPS

Put all the ingredients in a saucepan, bring
to the boil and simmer gently for 15 minutes
until thickened and reduced. Season to taste
with salt and pepper, then let cool completely.
Pour into a clean jar and store in the fridge
for up to five days.

FENNEL & MINT SLAW

2 heaped tbsp mayonnaise
freshly squeezed juice and grated
   zest of 1 lemon
200 g/7 oz. (about 1 small) fennel
   bulb, trimmed and sliced
   into rings
a bunch of fresh mint
40 g/scant 1 cup flat-leaf parsley
40 g/1½ oz. rocket/arugula
½ red onion, finely sliced

SERVES 6

To make the slaw, mix the
mayonnaise with the lemon
juice and zest and then dress
the fennel straight away to
prevent the fennel discolouring.
Gently mix through the herbs,
rocket and the red onion.

MANGO SALSA

2 mangos, peeled, pitted and
   very finely diced
1 long fresh red chilli/chile,
   deseeded and finely diced
1 tbsp chopped fresh coriander/
   cilantro
1 tbsp roughly chopped fresh
   mint leaves
½ medium red onion, finely diced
freshly squeezed juice of 1 lime
2 tsp palm sugar

SERVES 6

To make the salsa, mix all of the
ingredients together in a bowl
and set aside.

ROSEMARY COLESLAW

Because of its tangy, fresh taste, nothing goes with warm weather like homemade coleslaw. Along with hot dogs, cheeseburgers, BBQ baked beans and potato salad, it's a great component for a picnic or a get-together.

240 g/4 cups green or red cabbage, sliced or shredded thinly

1 large carrot, roughly grated

¼ medium red onion, chopped finely

1½ tsp sea salt, plus extra for seasoning

Dressing

60 g/¼ cup mayonnaise

60 g/¼ cup sour cream

1 tsp Dijon mustard

60 ml/¼ cup cider vinegar

¼ tsp caraway seeds

1 tsp fresh rosemary, chopped

1 small garlic clove, minced

pinch of cayenne pepper

1 tsp caster/granulated sugar

¼ tsp ground black pepper

pinch of sea salt

SERVES 4

Place the cabbage, carrot and onion in a large colander set over a large bowl or plate, sprinkle with salt and toss to coat. Place a heavy bowl on top of the cabbage, then place a heavy can or two in the bowl to weigh it down. Let it sit until the cabbage has released about 60 g/¼ cup of moisture, at least 1 hour.

Meanwhile, make the dressing. Add all the ingredients, except the sugar, pepper and salt to a large sterilized jar, screw the lid on securely and shake. Add the sugar, pepper and salt. Place the jar in the refrigerator for 30–60 minutes.

Transfer the cabbage, carrot and onion to a medium-size bowl and pour half the dressing over. Toss with tongs, cover and let the coleslaw sit for 30 minutes, tossing once or twice more to redistribute the dressing. Toss once more before serving and add additional dressing if desired. Leftover dressing will keep for up to 1 week in the refrigerator.

CLASSIC HAND-CUT FRIES

Although it might seem to some that fries should be prepared in a deep fryer, baking them in the oven delivers a better texture and crunch. It's also much easier to season them properly. These fries are crispy, golden and the perfect accompaniment to any burger. Eat them plain or dunk them in ketchup.

4 large baking potatoes
50 g/¼ cup olive oil
1 tbsp paprika
1 tbsp garlic powder
1 tbsp chilli/chili powder
1 tbsp onion powder

SERVES 4

Preheat the oven to 180°C (350°F) Gas 4.

Use a sharp knife to cut the potatoes into 2.5-cm/1-inch thick wedges. In a medium-size mixing bowl, mix together the olive oil, paprika, garlic powder, chilli powder and onion powder. Coat the potatoes in this oil and spice mixture and place them on a baking sheet.

Bake the fries for 45–60 minutes in the oven, turning once, and remove when they're golden and crispy.

SWEET POTATO FRIES

If you fancy a change from regular French fries, try this delicious alternative instead. The crisp, caramelized edge conceals a soft and sweet centre. This recipe calls for olive oil, but coconut oil can be used instead if you like.

4 sweet potatoes, cut to desired size and thickness

2–3 tbsp olive oil

1 tbsp salt

1 tbsp ground black pepper

¼ tsp cayenne pepper (optional)

2 large baking sheets, greased liberally with olive oil

SERVES 4

Preheat the oven to 200°C (400°F) Gas 6.

In a resealable plastic bag, combine the sweet potatoes, olive oil, salt, pepper and cayenne pepper, if using. Close and shake the bag until the sweet potatoes are evenly coated. Spread them out in a single layer on the two baking sheets.

Bake in the preheated oven for 30 minutes, or until the sweet potatoes are crispy and brown on one side. Turn the fries over using a spatula, and cook for another 30 minutes, or until they are all crispy on the outside and tender inside.

ALE-BATTERED ONION RINGS

Onion rings and French fries often compete for the title of main side dish. Although French fries are more common, it isn't until you have an onion ring in your mouth that you realize that if you were given the option, you would eat onion rings far more often.

120 g/1 cup plain/all-purpose flour, plus extra for dusting

250 ml/1 cup India pale ale

2 large brown or Vidalia onions

canola oil, for frying

salt, to taste

yellow mustard, to serve

Ranch dressing

250 ml/1 cup buttermilk, shaken

60 g/¼ cup mayonnaise

3 tsp sour cream

3 tbsp flat-leaf parsley, finely chopped

2 tbsp chives, finely chopped

4 tsp white wine vinegar or lemon juice

1 garlic clove, finely chopped

¼ tsp garlic powder

½ tsp sea salt

2 pinches ground black pepper

SERVES 4

First, make the ranch dressing. Put all the ingredients in a 500 ml/2 cup jar with a tight-fitting lid. Seal tightly and shake to evenly distribute all the ingredients. Check the seasoning and add additional salt and pepper as desired. Refrigerate until chilled and the flavours have melded, about 1 hour. The dressing will keep for up to 3 days in the refrigerator.

Put the flour into a mixing bowl and make a well in the centre. Pour the ale into the well and whisk until combined. Let the mixture rest, covered, for 1 hour.

Peel the onions and cut crosswise into 1-cm/⅓-inch thick rings. Dust the rings with more flour, shaking off the excess, and coat them with the batter.

Heat 5 cm/2 inches of canola oil in a large frying pan/skillet. The pan is at the right temperature when the oil is steadily bubbling. Working in batches, fry the onion rings until they're golden in colour. Use a slotted spoon to transfer the onion rings onto paper towels to drain. Sprinkle them with salt to taste.

Serve with yellow mustard and ranch dressing.

PICKLES

Pickles are a staple around the globe. These three pickles will keep for two weeks in the refrigerator. American Kool-Aid powder can be found online or in some stores.

SWEET & SOUR CHERRY PICKLES

½ jar Spicy Dill Pickles (see right), including the brine
1 packet cherry Kool-Aid powder
200 g/1 cup caster/granulated sugar

1 x sterilized 450 ml/16 oz. canning jar

MAKES 1 JAR

Follow the recipe to the right for Spicy Dill Pickles. After the brining is done, remove the pickles from the liquid. Stir the Kool-Aid and sugar in to the pickle brine until they have both dissolved. Add the pickles back to the mixture, and seal in the jar. Place in the refrigerator and let brine for at least 1 week before tasting.

SWEET PICKLES

240 ml/1 cup cider vinegar
40 g/⅛ cup salt
200 g/1 cup caster/granulated sugar
¼ tsp ground turmeric
½ tsp mustard seeds
400 g/14 oz. pickling cucumbers, quartered or halved and sliced lengthwise
1 sweet onion, sliced

2 x sterilized 450 ml/16 oz. canning jars

MAKES 2 JARS

In a saucepan over medium-high heat, combine the vinegar, salt, sugar, turmeric and mustard seeds. Bring to the boil and cook for 5 minutes. Loosely pack the cucumbers and onion into jars and pour the hot liquid over them. Remove air bubbles, wipe the rims and put the lids on. Let the cucumbers pickle for at least 24 hours before tasting.

SPICY DILL PICKLES

1 litre/4 cups water
300 ml/1¼ cups white vinegar
3 tbsp sea salt
8 dill sprigs
8 large garlic cloves
4 dried hot chilli/chile peppers
675 g/24 oz. pickling cucumbers, quartered or halved and sliced lengthways

4 x sterilized 450 ml/16 oz. canning jars

MAKES 4 JARS

In a stainless steel stockpot, bring the water, vinegar and salt to a boil. Let boil for 10–12 minutes.

Meanwhile, pack the cucumbers facing upwards into canning jars. Make sure they are at least 1.25 cm/½ inch below the jar's rim. Place 2 dill sprigs, 2 garlic cloves and 1 chilli in each jar. Carefully ladle the hot mixture into the jars. Add extra water if necessary so that the cucumbers are submerged, but leave 1.25 cm/½ inch of space from the rim of the jar. Remove air bubbles, wipe the rims and put the lids on. Let the cucumbers pickle for at least 24 hours before tasting.

INDEX

RECIPE CREDITS

MIRANDA BALLARD
Beef and Black Bean Sliders with Corn and Pepper Salsa
Beef and Mozzarella Sliders with Pesto Mayo and Rocket
Beef, Goat Cheese and Bean Burger with Pesto Mayo
Big Breakfast Burger with Portobello Mushroom and a Fried Egg
Chicken Caesar Sliders Wrapped in Parma Ham with Caesar Dressing
Chilli con Carne Burger
Classic Beef Burger with Tomato Ketchup and Lettuce
Curried Sweet Potato Burgers
Fish Pie Burger with Capers and Tartare Sauce
Hot and Smoky Barbecue Sauce
Indian-style Lamb Sliders with Minted Yogurt and Mango Chutney
Italian Burger with Olives, Sun-dried Tomatoes and Pesto
Mayos (Classic, Mustard, Herb, Lemon and Pesto)
Mexican Burger with Sour Cream, Salsa and Guacamole
Pulled Pork Shoulder
Spicy Beef and Pork Sliders with Ginger and Lime
Superfood Burgers
Ultimate Burger with Bacon, Cheese and Tomato Relish

AMY RUTH FINEGOLD
Quinoa Burgers with Portobello Mushrooms

DUNJA GULIN
Chunky Hummus Burgers
Spicy Vegan Burger and Wedges

CAROL HILKER
Ale-battered Onion Rings
Burnt Ends
Chilaquile Burger
Diner Cheeseburger
Handcut Fries
Pickles (Sweet and Sour, Sweet and Spicy Dill)
Rosemary Coleslaw
Sliders with Secret Sauce
Sweet Potato Fries

KATHY KORDALIS
Indian-spiced Cauli Burgers

JENNY LINFORD
Mushroom Burgers
Roast Garlic Pork Burgers

DAN MAY
Chilli Veggie Burger with Sun-dried Tomatoes and Spicy Red Onion Relish
Moroccan-spiced Lamb Burgers with Yogurt Dressing

THEO A. MICHAELS
Black Bean Burger
Southern Chicken Burgers with Cabbage and Lime Slaw

LOUISE PICKFORD
Bacon Burger with Sour Cream Slaw
Buffalo Cauliflower Burger with Blue Cheese Sauce
Chinese Crispy Duck Sliders with Hoisin and Spring Onions
Deep-fried Buttermilk Chicken Burger
Healthy Cod Burger with Watercress and Almond Pesto
Jamaican Jerk Tuna Burger with Tabasco Mayo
Japanese Salmon Katsu Sliders
Malaysian Prawn Sambal Sliders
Middle Eastern Sliders with Tahini Sauce
Thai Chicken Burger with Sweet Chilli Dressing
Turkey Burger with Onion and Cranberry Jam
Vietnamese Sesame Tofu Burger

JAMES PORTER
Teriyaki Burger

SHELAGH RYAN
Fennel and Mint Slaw
Mango Salsa
Spicy Pork Burger with Mango Salsa

LEAH VANDERVELDT
Black Bean and Beet Burgers

LAURA WASHBURN HUTTON
Chilli Ketchup
Curry Ketchup
Tomato Ketchup

PHOTOGRAPHY CREDITS

MARTIN BRIGDALE Pages 31, 35 and 81.

PETER CASSIDY Pages 11, 28, 29, 43, 47, 67, 68, 87, 100, 109, 119 and 123.

MOWIE KAY Pages 24, 55, 88, 91, 94, 95 and 115.

STEVE PAINTER Pages 16, 27, 36, 110–111, 112–113, 117, 119, 121, 122 and 124.

CHRISTOPHER SCHOLEY Page 10.

TOBY SCOTT Pages 2 and 60.

IAN WALLACE Pages 19, 32, 48, 49, 56, 63, 64, 71, 76, 83 and 99.

KATE WHITTAKER Pages 42, 52, 105 and 120.

CLARE WINFIELD Pages 1, 3, 5, 6, 9, 12, 13, 15, 20, 21, 23, 39, 44, 51, 57, 59, 72, 74, 75, 79, 80, 84, 96, 104, 107 and 114.